DRAMA CLASSICS

The Drama Classics series aims to offer the world's greatest plays in affordable paperback editions for students, actors and theatregoers. The hallmarks of the series are accessible introductions, uncluttered texts and an overall theatrical perspective.

Given that readers may be encountering a particular play for the first time, the introduction seeks to fill in the theatrical/historical background and to outline the chief themes rather than concentrate on interpretational and textual analysis. Similarly the play-texts themselves are free of footnotes and other interpolations: instead there is an end-glossary of 'difficult' words and phrases.

The texts of the English-language plays in the series have been prepared taking full account of all existing scholarship. The foreign-language plays have been newly translated into a modern English that is both actable and accurate: many of the translators regularly have their work staged professionally.

Edited until his early death by Kenneth McLeish, the Drama Classics series continues with his aim of providing a first-class library of dramatic literature representing the best of world theatre.

Associate editors:
Professor Trevor R. Griffiths
Dr. Colin Counsell
School of Arts and Humanities
University of North London

DRAMA CLASSICS *the first hundred*

*The publishers welcome
suggestions for further titles*

DRAMA CLASSICS

THREE SISTERS

by
Anton Chekhov

translated and introduced by
Stephen Mulrine

NICK HERN BOOKS
London
www.nickhernbooks.co.uk

A Drama Classic

Three Sisters first published in Great Britain in this translation as a paperback original in 1994 by Nick Hern Books Limited, 14 Larden Road, London W3 7ST

Reprinted 1999, 2000, 2002, 2003

Typeset by Country Setting, Kingsdown, Kent CT14 8ES
Printed in Great Britain by Bookmarque, Croydon, Surrey

A CIP catalogue record for this book is available from the British Library

ISBN 1 85459 221 1

Introduction

Anton Chekhov (1860-1904)

Anton Pavlovich Chekhov was born in Taganrog in South Russia, in 1860, just before the Emancipation, although his family had been bought out of serfdom some years earlier, by his paternal grandfather. By his own account, Chekhov's childhood was far from idyllic. His father Pavel was a domestic tyrant, fanatically religious, and Chekhov and his brothers were forced to rise before dawn to sing in the local church choir, then work long hours after school, minding the family grocery business.

Chekhov's record at the Taganrog school, not surprisingly, was undistinguished, and at the age of sixteen he was left behind to complete his education, when the family fled to Moscow to escape the consequences of his father's bankruptcy. In 1879, Chekhov entered Moscow University's Faculty of Medicine, and soon became the family's principal breadwinner, writing short comic pieces to supplement his student allowance.

By the time Chekhov qualified in 1884, his literary ambitions were already in conflict with what he regarded as his vocation, and indeed until his own health collapsed, he continued to practise medicine, mostly as an unpaid service. Chekhov was almost certainly infected with tuberculosis from childhood, and the disease was in its terminal stages before he would consent to a diagnosis. In addition to frequent haemorrhaging from the lungs, compelling him to spend the winters in the warm South, Chekhov suffered from a variety of other debilitating ailments, which make his work-rate little short of heroic. In 1899, when he sold the rights in his works to the publisher Marks, they already filled ten volumes, and the critical consensus is that his short stories represent an unparalleled achievement in the form, with the three great plays of his mature dramatic method scarcely less important.

Human relationships are the substance of his work, and it is perhaps no surprise that this most intimate of writers remained elusive in his own relationships. Fond of women, and pursued by several, Chekhov characteristically retreated as they advanced, and it is arguable that the happiness of his brief married life, with the actress Olga Knipper, depended on the lengthy periods of separation forced on the couple by Chekhov's poor health, and Olga's busy metropolitan career.

Finally, in an effort to postpone the inevitable, Chekhov travelled with Olga to Germany for medical treatment, and in July 1904, following a heart attack, he died in the spa town of Badenweiler, at the age of forty-four.

Three Sisters: **What Happens in the Play**

To write a play exploring a situation in which 'nothing happens' is to risk being accused of writing a play in which nothing happens. This has been Chekhov's fate with *Three Sisters:* critics used to condemn the play as formless, actionless, plotless – any kind of 'less' they could think of. In fact it is tightly controlled, as precise in its effects as poetry, as organised as chamber music. Rather than revealing the situation in a narrative way, Chekhov sets it out whole and then explores it detail by detail: it is as if we were experiencing a painting or a tapestry, and the play's momentum depends as much on gradual discovery, inexorable revelation, as on plot-'surprises' or consequentiality.

Olga, Masha and Irina Prozorov are three sisters, daughters of a recently dead general in a remote battalion town. They are upper-middle-class, and feel stifled by the dullness of their provincial environment. They dream of moving to the sophistication and intellectual and emotional fulfilment of Moscow. In the meantime, Olga parcels out her time as an overworked headmistress, Masha is trapped in a stifling marriage to the boring schoolmaster Kulygin, and Irina has a dead-end job in the Post Office. The sister's weak-willed brother Andrei marries a local girl, Natalya, and part of the story involves the way her ferocious ambition and energy becomes more and more at odds with the sisters' genteel, conventional and more kindly outlook on life.

If the situation revolves round the growing tension between Natalya and the sisters (and Andrei's unhappiness and bafflement as he watches it), the action also involves attempts to break out, to fulfil themselves, by Masha and Irina. Masha begins a love-affair with Vershinin, a colonel in the garrison – but it comes to nothing when the regiment is moved on and he leaves her. Irina engages herself to a man she doesn't love, Baron Tuzenbakh – but he is killed in a pointless duel. Other characters include two popinjay second lieutenants, Fedotik and Rode, the elderly army doctor Chebutykin, who escapes the dreariness of life by drinking, and the elderly nurse Anfisa, one of the principal targets of Natalya's zeal for change.

In the counterpoint of images and ideas which ally the play's structure to music, two themes are particularly prominent. Tuzenbakh and Vershinin have long conversations, what Chekhov calls 'philosophising', about how much better life may be 200 years from now, and the metaphor of bird-migration constantly reappears. We humans are like birds, busy about our lives, but underlying everything is the unexplained, unexplainable urge to to take flight, to migrate from this daily existence to another – and if this is not acknowledged, or is frustrated, our existence can become insupportable.

Chekhov the Dramatist

Chekhov might be described as *par excellence* the writer's writer, not only on account of his work, or the fund of wisdom in his correspondence, ranging from points of principle to technical wrinkles, but also the example he presents of the restless self-improver, grinding his way over a mere two decades from penny-a-line squibs in the Russian equivalent of 'Tit-Bits', to the status of modern classic, in both his preferred genres.

In that respect, the year 1887-88 represents a turning-point in his career, with the production in November 1887 of his first four-act play, *Ivanov*, and the publication, in March the following year, of his short story 'The Steppe' in one of the prestige 'thick journals', "The Northern Herald". The same year also witnessed his official recognition as a major Russian writer with the award of the Pushkin Prize by the Academy of

Sciences. Chekhov had arrived, though the extraordinary reception given to the Moscow première of *Ivanov*, greeted with mixed cheering and booing, suggested that he had arrived as a dramatist some way ahead of his audience.

Indeed, that is broadly the story of Chekhov's dramatic career, and it is significant that the main bone of contention in *Ivanov*, dividing first-nighters into partisans and scoffers, was the author's seeming abdication of any clear moral stance with respect to the play's 'anti-hero' Ivanov and its voice of conscience, the self-righteous Dr Lvov. After some changes, however, the play was successfully revived in St.Petersburg, and Chekhov was sufficiently encouraged by the experience to offer *The Wood Demon* for production in Moscow the following year. Alas, *The Wood Demon* was a flop, and in the light of Chekhov's developing method, it is interesting to note that criticism generally centred on its lack of action and dreary, slice-of-life dialogue. Chekhov withdrew the play in disgust, and buried it deep within his mysterious creative processes, whence it re-surfaced in 1898, in the radically altered form of *Uncle Vanya*, one of the greatest works of the modern theatre.

In between times, in 1896, Chekhov had also endured the catastrophic failure of *The Seagull*, an experience which encapsulated almost everything that was wrong with the Russian theatre he inherited, and which his work did so much to change. *The Seagull* was premièred in October 1896 at the Alexandrinsky Theatre in St.Petersburg, having spent almost a year in the hands of the censors, and the actors received their scripts a bare week before opening night. The play had been commissioned from Chekhov in the belief that it would be a fitting vehicle for the benefit performance of one of the

Alexandrinsky's stars, a mature comedienne with a large and vociferous following.

For most Russians, Chekhov's reputation was still that of 'Antosha Chekhonte', the comic journalist of the previous decade, and while *The Seagull* is undoubtedly more robust than Stanislavsky's later interpretation, it is very far from the broad comedy Madame Levkeyev's fans were expecting. She had originally been billed to play Arkadina, and disappointment at her non-appearance soon gave way to whistling and jeering, from Nina's Act One monologue as the 'World Spirit' onwards.

Not for the first or last time, Chekhov's irony escaped the play's more sober critics, who affected to believe that Konstantin's absurd symbolist playlet represented the new form of theatre that his creator sought. *The Seagull* is a transitional work, nonetheless, and in that regard it is notable that the Alexandrinsky Theatre Committee, despite accepting the play for production, expressed reservations about its 'Ibsenism' – a comparison Chekhov would not have relished.

After the fiasco of *The Seagull*, Chekhov virtually fled from St. Petersburg, and although the play's fortunes improved with 'normal' audiences, for the remainder of its brief run, the generally hostile reviews made him resolve to quit the theatre for ever. Fortunately, the first great play of his mature dramatic method, *Uncle Vanya*, appears to have been nearing completion by this time, and while the course of its development out of *The Wood Demon* remains shrouded in mystery, it is difficult to believe that it could have preceded *The Seagull*. At any rate, *Uncle Vanya* first surfaced in 1897, when Chekhov included it in a published collection of his plays.

The following year, 1898, saw the coming together of Chekhov and the directors of the newly-founded Moscow Art Theatre – a union commonly presented as a marriage made in theatre heaven. Both parties shared an intense dissatisfaction with the Russian theatre of the day, its bombastic acting, poor technical standards, and outmoded star system. What Chekhov's plays needed – natural, unforced speaking, even-handed ensemble playing and meticulous rehearsal, led by sensitive interpretation – appeared to be exactly what Stanislavsky and Nemirovich-Danchenko could bring to them. And if the marriage turned out to be less than wholly blissful, it is to their credit, nonetheless, that Chekhov continued to write for the theatre, including the two masterpieces specially commissioned by the Moscow Art Theatre, *Three Sisters* and *The Cherry Orchard*.

Chekhov had in fact written to Nemirovich-Danchenko in November 1896, soon after the Alexandrinsky première of *The Seagull*, and his own words best describe the trauma he had experienced: " The theatre breathed malice, the very air was compressed with hatred, and in accordance with the laws of physics, I shot out of St. Petersburg like a bomb!" Not surprisingly, Chekhov's health took a severe downturn at this point, and by the time Nemirovich-Danchenko had managed to convince both Chekhov and his co-director Stanislavsky that the new company, already ailing, should stage *The Seagull*, the pattern of Chekhov's relationships with the Moscow Art Theatre was effectively set – fleeting visits for readthroughs and rehearsals, fine tuning by correspondence, and the tense wait by the phone for news of the opening. Indeed, not until 1900, when the Moscow Art Theatre visited Yalta, did Chekhov see the company perform his work.

The rapturous reception accorded to *The Seagull*, at its Moscow première on the 17th of December 1898, has of course passed into theatre legend, as have Chekhov's disagreements, with Stanislavsky in particular, over the interpretation of his work. In general terms, Stanislavsky tended to over-direct the plays, often imposing a sentimental colouring on Chekhov's characters, and detailing their physical environment too precisely through his notorious noises-off. What the Moscow Art Theatre did give Chekhov, however, was adequate rehearsal – twelve weeks for *The Seagull*, for example – and indeed the company's legacy can be seen in the extravagant run-up times, and autocratic direction, of much Russian theatre still.

The success of *The Seagull* not only restored Chekhov's confidence, it also rescued the Moscow Art Theatre, and the company were eager to attempt *Uncle Vanya*, which had already been staged in the provinces, following its publication the previous year. Unfortunately, Chekhov had promised the play to the prestigious Maly Theatre, but the script changes being demanded by its literary committee gave him a legitimate excuse for withdrawing the offer, and *Uncle Vanya* was duly produced by the Moscow Art Theatre in October 1899 – in terms of its reception, more consolidation than triumph, perhaps, but sufficiently encouraging to focus Chekhov's mind on the subject he had already identified for a wholly new work – the lives of three sisters, daughters of the garrison, in a remote provincial town.

Chekhov arrived in Moscow with the completed manuscript of *Three Sisters* the following October, but his first readthrough with the actors, including Olga Knipper (whom he was soon to marry, and for whom he had designed the role of Masha) ran into predictable difficulties over his intention, and crucial questions of tone. During the winter months, which Chekhov's deteriorating health compelled him to spend in Nice, he continued to revise *Three Sisters*, and attempted, at long range, to restrain Stanislavsky's exuberance – though to do him justice, the director swiftly dropped his original plan to have Tuzenbakh's corpse ferried across the stage after the Act Four duel!

Chekhov was still out of the country when *Three Sisters* opened, in January 1901, and while it was certainly no failure, neither it, nor *The Cherry Orchard* three years later, managed to repeat the smash hit of *The Seagull*. Chekhov was bitterly disappointed, but in each case, the longer the plays ran, the better the audience response, and a revival of *Three Sisters* in Moscow the following season successfully established it in the repertoire.

By the spring of 1903, when he at last committed *The Cherry Orchard* to paper, Chekhov had little more than a year left to live, and required some persistent coaxing by Olga Knipper and Stanislavsky to have the play ready for the next season. When the Moscow Art Theatre did finally receive the script in October, Stanislavsky's effusive account of how he had dissolved in tears, reading what Chekhov insisted was a comedy, can scarcely have extended the author's life.

Chekhov's theatre, of course, had outstripped the terminology available to him, and despite its genuine achievement, Stanislavsky's still bore traces of the overblown, melodramatic tradition it had been created to supplant. Chekhov's instructions to Stanislavsky, throughout the period of their association, amount to a plea for understatement, for a lightness of touch foreign to the actor-director's instincts.

Indeed, it may be suspected that the growing audience for the Moscow Art Theatre's Chekhov, then and later, more readily understood and empathised with the tragic somnambulists of Stanislavsky's interpretation, than the robust complexity of Chekhov's own vision.

Certainly, that was Mayakovsky's judgment, less than a generation after Chekhov's death, when he poured scorn on this bloodless theatre, with its 'Auntie Manyas and Uncle Vanyas lolling on the settee', but that was no fault of Chekhov's, who was scarcely more enchanted by his gallery of *fainéants* than was Mayakovsky. That is quite a different matter from the enchantment of the plays themselves, which remains a constant through changing interpretations – and that same oblique, low-key rhetoric, which challenged his original audiences, allows us to hear Chekhov still as among the most modern voices of the classic drama repertoire.

Three Sisters

Chekhov describes *Three Sisters* as a 'drama', the only play he so designates, and in a letter written soon after its completion, he speaks of it having 'an atmosphere more gloomy than gloom itself'. Its central theme, that of the creeping usurpation of the Prozorovs' house and patrimony by Natasha, is prefigured in a short story of 1899, 'In the Ravine', in which the lively and industrious Aksinya eventually drives her husband's family out of their own house, having earlier killed her sister-in-law's baby in an act of casual savagery. Aksinya also has a long-running affair with a local mill-owner, and there are enough other similiarities between this grimly un-Tolstoyan peasant idyll and *Three Sisters* to suggest that

Chekhov was revisiting the subject for his first Moscow Art Theatre commission.

Three Sisters is, however, a masterpiece of free-standing construction, and even the most cursory inspection of its intricate mechanisms, the complex interconnected lives of its ten major players, gives the lie to the persistent notion that Chekhov's drama lacks plot. In abstract terms, there is an element of folk-tale symmetry about the play, and it is perhaps not too fanciful to extend this to a crude typology of the sisters themselves – the solidly domestic Olga, the sensual Masha, the virginal Irina – like facets of some idealised Woman. These, and the relentless forward movement of the play, as Natasha colonises room after room in the Prozorov house, furnish the scaffolding of *Three Sisters*, but Chekhov's is an art of concealment, such that we are aware only of the detail, the civilised table-talk for the most part, of a community in which on-stage violence is represented by Natasha's rudeness to the servants, while Masha and Vershinin conduct their extra-marital indiscretions for the most part in discreet code.

Chekhov's declared intention was to banish 'drama' to the wings, and *Three Sisters* achieves this in more than the off-stage pistol shot which wrecks Irina's hopes. Protopopov, for example, a prime mover in the sisters' downhill slide, appears only by passing mention – the absent cake-giver at Irina's name-day party, Natasha's gentleman caller, in his waiting troika, little Sophie's babysitter, and putative father, when the usurpation is finally complete. Protopopov's cake, in the context of later developments, has a distinctly bitter aftertaste.

Likewise, in a play which repeatedly exposes the gap between the characters' pretensions and their true situation, the off-stage presence of Vershinin's wife and daughters subtly undermines his credibility, though he is as much of a hero as the play can muster. Despite his charm, and the ringing optimism of his 'philosophising', the last word on Vershinin is not Masha's, but rather his own request to Olga, to watch over his emotional left luggage for a month or two, until he's settled into the next garrison town, with doubtless another flower-filled room in the offing.

Moreover, the telling contribution, in Chekhov's drama, of unseen characters is matched by that of unspoken lines and implicit connections. Tuzenbakh's final conversation with Irina, for example, is achingly incomplete, and not only because of what he must conceal. In a play which wears its plot lightly, there is scarcely a word or deed, however casual-seeming, that is not purposefully linked to another. Thus Natasha's grand design, mistress of all she surveys, to cut down the Prozorovs' cherished trees and plant flowers in their stead, recalls not only Tuzenbakh's emotional farewell to those same trees a short while before, but also Vershinin's first impressions of the Prozorov house, interior and exterior, at the beginning of the play.

Again, the sisters' unkind observations on Natasha's dress sense come full circle in the final Act, when she repays the compliment to Irina. Much of our sympathy, indeed, is engaged by Irina, but she is a particular focus of Chekhov's irony, just as she most embodies the sisters' illusory hopes. Is it possible, for example, as she finally dedicates her life to teaching, that she can have forgotten her elder sister's experience?

In the light of later developments, the serial debate between the two amateur futurologists, Vershinin and Tuzenbakh, holds a particular fascination, and Chekhov has suffered from attempts to locate the author's voice in this work especially. On balance, if there is a message to be got from the *totality* of the play, as distinct from individual speeches, then that is most plausibly presented in Tuzenbakh's analysis of an existence whose laws we cannot fathom, and which will remain fundamentally unchanged, in all but the most superficial details.

That is not to deny hope, and indeed the very rhythms of Vershinin's great operatic arias surely convey the intensity of Chekhov's feeling. However, hope is not faith, and the author's belief (as articulated more reliably, perhaps, in his letters) is coloured by his own experience of the left and right ideologues of the day. Chekhov's vision, indeed, set out in a famous letter to the poet Pleshcheyev, of a Russia which, 'Beneath the banner of science, art and oppressed freedom of thought . . . will one day be ruled by toads and crocodiles, of a sort unknown even in Spain under the Inquisition . . . ' is infinitely more chilling than Tuzenbakh's 'fierce, cleansing wind', to which the twentieth century has supplied its own sub-text. Tuzenbakh seeks salvation through toil in a brick-works, and Solzhenitsyn's first labour camp, at 'New Jerusalem' on the outskirts of Moscow, was a brickyard, an irony which he develops at some length in the second volume of the 'Gulag Archipelago'.

Despite that, the experience of *Three Sisters* in the theatre is both intensely moving and uplifting. The sisters' closing speeches, however they may appear to be subverted by Chebutykin's killing indifference, represent a hymn to human endurance scarcely to be matched in the modern theatre. Of course we know that even if Chekhov's people were to achieve their hearts' desire, it would turn instantly to ashes. What model, for example, does he offer of domestic bliss that any of his characters, Natasha included, should even contemplate marriage? As for Andrei's academic yearnings, the career of Serebryakov, in *Uncle Vanya*, or the narrator's reflections in 'A Boring Story', hint at the likely outcome, in Chekhov's world, had Andrei satisfied that ambition.

The sisters' Moscow, the repository of all their hopes, is likewise a dream landscape, a symbol of the unattainable, and Irina's outburst, to the effect that there's no place like Moscow on this earth, is comical even without benefit of hindsight. Among the major characters, in fact, only the rapacious Natasha actually lives in the present, or realises her aims. She is happy and fulfilled, in the manner of a predatory animal sleeping off a successful kill on some featureless provincial prairie.

It is that very gulf, between aspiration and realisation, into which we pour our sympathy for Chekhov's often absurd characters; it is the piercing view he affords us of our own plight that moves us, and Stanislavsky's tears were scarcely out of place, even if the playing demands a healthy comic detachment. And in the long run, Chekhov's bleakest play still warms us with the consolation of love, the deep affection of the sisters, shining out like a beacon from the play's closing tableau.

The Language

Literary Russian has undergone much less change since Chekhov's day than English, and there is scant justification for affecting a period style in translation, particularly with a writer whose stated aim was to bring conversation to the stage, the common speech of the educated classes of his day, uttered in more or less commonplace contexts. As a stylist, he derives ultimately from the tradition of Pushkin, that of spare, economical writing, and his letters to Gorky, chiding the latter for his verbosity, define his ideal by default. That is not to say, however, that Chekhov cannot deliver a rolling peroration when the occasion demands, and the 'visionary' speeches of Vershinin, Tuzenbakh, even Irina and Andrei, are among the most compelling writing for the stage this century.

The Translation

Apart from those endemic to the medium, the translation of *Three Sisters* presents some peculiar problems through Chekhov's occasional use of snatches of song and poetry, and a few of these warrant a separate note. Thus, in Act One, Masha quotes the opening lines of the prologue to Pushkin's mock-heroic poem 'Ruslan and Lyudmila', familiar to every educated Russian: "By a curving shore stands a green oak tree/Bound by a golden chain . . . " The unspoken next line of Pushkin's poem introduces a learned cat, doubtless a concealed ironic hit at Kulygin, and Masha's marital fetters, but she does not refer to the cat until Act Four, and then only in a garbled form.

Soliony's lines: 'Before he had time to gasp/The bear had him in its grasp . . . ' come from a fable by the Russian Aesop, Ivan Krylov, titled 'The Peasant and the Workman', and in Act Three, Soliony again quotes Krylov: 'This moral I might make more clear/But that would vex the geese, I fear', from his fable 'The Geese'. Soliony's lines in Act Two: 'I am strange, but who is not? Be not angry, Aleko!', and 'Forget, forget thy dreams!', roll together a quotation from Griboyedov's verse comedy *Woe from Wit*, and a reference to the hero of Pushkin's poem, 'The Gipsies', although not a direct quotation. The Captain's pretensions as a latter-day Lermontov incline him to utterances of this kind, and he aptly dramatises his own exit to fight the duel with the concluding lines of Lermontov's poem 'The Sail': 'But he, rebellious, seeks the storm/As if in storms lay peace . . . ' Pushkin's 'Eugene Onegin', or rather the Tchaikovsky libretto, is the source of Vershinin's lines, 'To Love all ages humbly bow/Her promptings do each heart endow', sung in the opera by Gremin, celebrating love in the autumn of one's life.

Chebutykin is also much given to quoting snatches of song, and his lines: 'For love alone did Nature/Bring us forth upon this earth', in Act One, and "Oh, lady, please accept this fruit', ('date' in the Russian) in Act Three, derive from forgotten operettas. His insouciant 'Ta-ra-ra-boom-dee-ay' in Act Four tempts the translator with a second line, which means literally 'I'm sitting on a kerbstone', but it's perhaps best simply repeated, as in the original song. Near the end of Act Two, Tuzenbakh, Chebutykin and Andrei join in a traditional folk ditty about a new maplewood porch, difficult to translate, and impossible to sing, and I have left it as a stage direction. The bizarre exchange in the same Act, over

Chebutykin's meal of 'chekhartmá', which Soliony wilfully mishears as 'cheremshá', might have come from Ionesco, but the Caucasian words mean what each claims, and are as exotic in Russian as they are in English.

On the question of Russian patronymics and diminutives, I have followed a policy of compromise – Irina ought to address Chebutykin with a degree of formality, hence 'Ivan Romanych'. On the other hand, she rebuffs the advances of 'Captain Soliony' in this version, and not 'Vasily Vasilich', for ease of speaking. Similarly I have retained the Russian affectionate diminutive on occasion: 'Andryusha', for example, sounds particularly unctuous on Natasha's lips, but in general I have paraphrased, so that Anfisa, for example, refers to 'my lovely Olya', rather than 'Olyushka'.

Pronunciation

Where the stress in English names regularly falls on the penultimate syllable, Russian stress, which is also heavier, is much less predictable, and this gives rise to pronunciation difficulties, quite apart from its unfamiliar consonant clusters. The following is an approximation only of those names and words which might present difficulty in the spoken text, in order of their appearance, with the stressed syllables clearly marked:

Andrei: Ahn*dray*
Vershinin: Ver*shee*nin
Ivan Romanych: Ee*vahn* Ro*mah*nitch
Dobrolyubov: Dobro*lyoo*boff
Protopopov: Proto*paw*poff
Ferapont: Fera*pawnt*
Mikhail PotapychMee*khail* ('ai' pronounced 'eye') Po*tah*pitch
Ivanych: Ee*vah*nitch
Prozorov: *Proh*zoroff
Ignatyevich, Ignatych: Ig*nah*tyevitch, Ig*nah*titch
Olga Sergeyevna: *Awl*ga Ser*gay*evna ('gay' as English)
Basmanny: Bass*mah*ny
Nemetsky: Nyeh*met*sky
Krasny: *Krahss*ny
Soliony: Sol*yaw*ny
Novo-Devichy: *Nauvo*-*Dyeh*vitchy
Andryusha: An*dryoo*sha
Sergeyich: Ser*gay*itch
Kulygin: Koo*lee*ghin

Fyodor: *Fyaw*dor
Irina Sergeyevna: Ee*ree*na Ser*gay*evna
Ivan Romanych: Ee*vahn* Ro*mah*nitch
Bobik: *Baw*bik
Tyestov: *Tyeh*stoff
Saratov: Sa*rah*toff
Berdichev: Ber*deet*cheff
Tsitsikar: Tseetsee*kahr*
Anfisa: An*fee*sa
Aleko: Al*yeh*ko
Lermontov: *Lehr*montoff
cheremsha: cherem*shah*
chekhartma: chekhart*mah*
Kirsanov: Keer*sah*noff
Fedotik: Fe*daw*tik
Kolotilin: Kolo*teel*in
Zasyp: *Zah*sip
Rodé: Raw*day*
Kohane: Ko*hah*nay
Kozyrev: *Kawzir*yeff
Skvortsov: Skvort*sohff*
'Papa' and 'Mama': accented on the first syllable.

For Further Reading

Among the several biographies of Chekhov, Ronald Hingley's
A New Life of Chekhov, Oxford University Press, 1976, is
outstanding not only for its wealth of detail, and brisk, lively
narrative, but also for the care the author takes to disentangle
the man from the work. *Anton Chekhov Rediscovered* (eds.
Senderovich and Sendich), published by the Russian
Language Journal, 1987, contains a comprehensive
bibiography of works in English about and by Chekhov, as
well as a perceptive study of communication in *Three Sisters*.
A Chekhov Companion, ed. Toby W. Clyman, Greenwood Press,
1985, is a valuable collection, with articles on themes ranging
from social conditions in late 19th century Russia, through
the critical tradition, both native and Western, to Chekhov in
performance and translation, and Patrick Miles' little book
Chekhov on the British Stage 1909-1987, published by Sam &
Sam, is also useful.

Chekhov: Key Dates

1860   Born 17 January in Taganrog, a port on the Sea of Azov.

1875   Father's grocery business fails, family flees to Moscow, leaving Chekhov behind to complete his education.

1879   Graduates from the local high school, and leaves for Moscow, enters the Medical Faculty of Moscow University.

1880   First comic story published in *The Dragonfly*, a St. Petersburg weekly.

1884   Graduates from the University, begins medical practice.

1885   Begins contributing short stories to the *St. Petersburg Gazette* and *New Time*.

1886   First collection, *Motley Stories*.

1887   Second collection, *In the Twilight*, Awarded Pushkin Prize the following year, by the Imperial Academy of Sciences.

1887   First performance of *Ivanov* at Korsh's Theatre, Moscow, 19 November.

1888   First major story, 'The Steppe', published in a prestigious literary journal, the *Northern Herald*.

1889   First performance of *The Wood Demon* at Abramov's Theatre, Moscow, 27 December.

1890   Travels across Siberia to carry out research on the penal colony of Sakhalin Island.

1896   First, disastrous performance of *The Seagull*, at the Alexandrinsky Theatre in St. Petersburg, 17 October.

1898   Begins association with the Moscow Art Theatre. Worsening tuberculosis forces him to move to Yalta. On 17 December, first successful performance of *The Seagull*, by the Moscow Art Theatre.

1899   First Moscow performance of *Uncle Vanya*, by the same company, 26 October.

1901   First performance of *Three Sisters*, 31 January. Marries the actress Olga Knipper.

1903   Publishes last story, 'The Betrothed'.

1904   First performance of *The Cherry Orchard*, 17 January. Dies in Badenweiler, Germany, 2 July.

THREE SISTERS

Dramatis Personae

PROZOROV, Andrei Sergeyevich.
NATALYA IVANOVNA, his fiancée, later his wife.
OLGA }
MASHA } his sisters.
IRINA }
KULYGIN, Fyodor Ilyich, a high school teacher,
   Masha's husband.
VERSHININ, Aleksandr Ignatyevich, Lieut. Colonel,
   battery commander.
TUZENBAKH, Nikolai Lvovich, Baron, Lieutenant.
SOLIONY, Vasily Vasilyevich, Staff Captain.
CHEBUTYKIN, Ivan Romanovich, military doctor.
FEDOTIK, Aleksei Petrovich, Second Lieutenant.
RODE, Vladimir Karlovich, Second Lieutenant.
FERAPONT, the local council watchman, an old man
ANFISA, nurse, an old woman of eighty.

The action takes place in a provincial town.

Act One

The PROZOROVS' *house. A drawing-room with pillars, behind which can be seen a large ballroom. It is mid-day, bright and sunny. In the ballroom, the table is being set for lunch.* OLGA *is wearing the blue uniform dress of a teacher at the girls' high school, and while she stands and moves around, she corrects exercise books;* MASHA, *in a black dress, sits with her hat in her lap, reading a book.* IRINA, *dressed in white, stands deep in thought.*

OLGA. Father died exactly a year ago, this very day. On your name-day, Irina, the fifth of May. It was very cold then – snowing. I thought I'd never get over it, and you had fainted, lying as if you were dead. And here we are, a year's gone by, and we can talk about it quite calmly. You're wearing white again, looking radiant . . .

A clock strikes twelve.

The clock struck then too.

A pause.

And I remember, when they carried father out, the band was playing, and they fired a salute at the graveside. He was a general, a brigade commander, yet so few people came to the funeral. Still, it was raining. Heavy rain, and sleet.

IRINA. Why bring it all back?

In the ballroom, beyond the pillars, BARON TUZENBAKH,

CHEBUTYKIN *and* SOLIONY *appear at the table.*

OLGA. It's warm today, we can even have the windows open, and the birch-trees still aren't out. Father got his brigade, and we left Moscow eleven years ago, yet I can remember so well, how everything's already in flower in Moscow by this time, the beginning of May, how warm it is, everything bathed in sunlight. Yes, eleven years have passed, and I remember it all, as if we'd left only yesterday. Oh, dear God – I woke up this morning, saw the light streaming in, the spring sunshine, and felt such joy welling up in my heart, such an intense longing to go home.

CHEBUTYKIN. Oh, forget it!

TUZENBAKH. It's nonsense, of course.

MASHA, *absorbed in her book, begins softly whistling.*

OLGA. Masha, stop whistling. How can you?

A pause.

Yes, I daresay it's because I'm at school all day, and then in the evening I have to give lessons, but my head aches the whole time, and I've already started to think like an old woman. To tell you the truth, these past four years I've been teaching at the high school, it's as if all my strength and youth have been ebbing away, drop by drop. The only thing that grows and gets stronger, is the one dream I have . . .

IRINA. To go to Moscow! To sell this house, leave it all behind, and head for Moscow . . .

OLGA. Oh, yes! To Moscow, as soon as possible!

CHEBUTYKIN *and* TUZENBAKH *laugh.*

IRINA. Our brother'll no doubt be a professor – in any case he won't go on living here. There's only one snag, and that's poor Masha.

OLGA. Masha can come to Moscow for the whole summer, every year.

MASHA *is still softly whistling.*

IRINA. God willing, it'll all work out. (*Looking out of the window.*) What a beautiful day it is. I don't know why, I just feel so light-hearted! This morning I remembered it was my name-day, and I suddenly felt so happy. I remembered when I was little, and Mama was still alive. Oh, and such wonderful thoughts came into my mind, such feelings!

OLGA. You're looking radiant today, even more beautiful than usual. And Masha's beautiful too. Andrei could be quite handsome, except he's got so stout, and it doesn't suit him. And I've grown old and terribly thin, I suppose from losing my temper with the girls at school. Still, I have a day off today, I'm at home, my headache's gone, and I feel younger than I did yesterday. Twenty-eight, that's all I am . . . Everything's fine, it's God's will, but even so – I think I'd have done better if I'd got married and stayed home all day.

A pause.

Yes, I'd have loved my husband.

TUZENBAKH (*to* SOLIONY). Honestly, you talk such nonsense, I'm fed up listening to you. (*Entering the drawing-room.*) By the way, I forgot to mention. You'll be having a visit today from our new battery commander, Vershinin. (*He sits down at the piano.*)

OLGA. Really? That'll be nice.

IRINA. Is he old?

TUZENBAKH. No, not particularly. He's about forty, forty-five at most. (*He begins to play, softly.*) He's a decent chap, by all accounts. He's no fool, that's for sure. Talks too much, though.

IRINA. Is he an interesting person?

TUZENBAKH. Yes, I suppose so. He's got a wife, mind you, and a mother-in-law and two little girls. Married for the second time, no less. Pays calls on everybody, tells them he's got a wife and two little girls. He'll say it here too. His wife's a bit cracked, wears her hair in a long braid, like a schoolgirl, talks all sorts of pretentious rot, philosophy and so on. Keeps trying to commit suicide, obviously to spite him. I'd have cleared off long ago, but he sticks it out, just complains.

SOLIONY (*entering from the dining room, with* CHEBUTYKIN). Now, with one hand, I can lift fifty pounds – but with two, a hundred and eighty, possibly two hundred. And from that I conclude that two men aren't just twice as strong as one, but three times, or even more . . .

CHEBUTYKIN (*reading a newspaper as he enters*). For falling hair . . . nine grammes of naphthalene in a half-bottle of alcohol . . . to be dissolved, and applied daily . . . (*He writes in a notebook.*) Better jot that down! (*To* SOLIONY.) So anyway, as I was telling you, you put a cork into a little bottle, and pass a glass tube through it . . . Then you take just a pinch of common-or-garden alum . . .

IRINA. Ivan Romanych, dearest Ivan Romanych!

CHEBUTYKIN. My dear, sweet child, what is it?

IRINA. Tell me, why am I so happy today? It's as if I'm sailing, with a wide deep sky above me and great white birds flying past. Why is that? Tell me, why?

CHEBUTYKIN (*kisses both her hands, tenderly*). My little white bird . . .

IRINA. When I woke up this morning, I got up and washed, and it was as if everything in this life had suddenly become clear to me, and I knew how I ought to live. Dear Ivan Romanych, I know everything now. A man must labour, he should work in the sweat of his brow, no matter who he is, and that's the only thing that gives meaning and purpose to his life, the source of all his happiness and joy. Oh, it must be wonderful to be a workman, and get up when it's still barely light, to break stones on the road, or a shepherd, or a teacher, teaching children, or an engine-driver on the railway . . . Dear God, better to be a dumb ox, or a horse, if only to work – anything but a girl who gets up at twelve o'clock, takes her coffee in bed, then spends two hours dressing! That's awful! It's like having a terrible thirst in a heatwave, that's how much I long to work. And if I don't get up early, and really work, well then, Ivan Romanych, you can just refuse to be my friend.

CHEBUTYKIN (*tenderly*). That's exactly what I'll do.

OLGA. Father trained us to get up at seven. Nowadays Irina wakes at seven, and then lies thinking until at least nine o'clock. And with such a serious face! (*Laughs.*)

IRINA. You're so used to seeing me as a little girl – you think it's strange if I look serious. But I'm twenty!

TUZENBAKH. This longing for work – dear God, it's all so
    familiar! I've never done a stroke of work in my life. I was
    born in St.Petersburg, a cold, listless town, to a family
    that'd never known either work, or want. I remember I
    used to come home from the cadet corps, and a
    manservant had to pull off my boots; I'd be acting the
    goat, while my mother looked on admiringly; she just
    couldn't believe other people saw me in a different light.
    No, they shielded me from work. But they only just
    managed it, yes indeed! The time has come, the storm
    clouds are massing for all of us, a fierce, cleansing wind's
    blowing up, it's coming, it's not far away, and it's going to
    sweep the idleness right out of our society, all the apathy,
    and prejudice against work, the rotten boredom. I shall
    work, yes, and in twenty-five or thirty years' time,
    everybody'll work. Every one of us!

CHEBUTYKIN. Well, I shan't work.

TUZENBAKH. You don't count.

SOLIONY. In twenty-five years' time you won't even be alive,
    thank God. In another couple of years you'll die of a
    stroke. Either that or I'll lose my temper and plant a bullet
    in your brain, my angel. (*He takes a little bottle of scent from
    his pocket and sprinkles some on his chest and hands.*)

CHEBUTYKIN (*laughs*). Well, I've never done a thing,
    I must say. Since I left university, I haven't so much as
    lifted a finger, haven't read a single book, nothing but
    newspapers . . . (*He takes another newspaper out of his pocket.*)
    Look, see . . . I know from the papers that there was
    somebody called Dobrolyubov, but what he wrote about,
    I haven't a clue. God knows . . .

Someone knocks up from downstairs.

Ah! They're calling me down, someone's come to see me. I'll be back in a minute . . . wait there . . . (*He hurriedly exits, stroking his beard.*)

IRINA. He's up to something.

TUZENBAKH. Yes. He's gone off with such a pompous look on his face, he's obviously about to bring in your present.

IRINA. Oh, I hate that!

OLGA. Yes, it's awful. He's always doing something silly.

MASHA. 'By a curving shore stands a green oak tree, Bound with a golden chain . . . Bound with a golden chain . . . '

She rises, and begins to hum softly.

OLGA. You're not very cheerful today, Masha.

MASHA, *still humming, puts on her hat.*

Where are you going?

MASHA. Home.

IRINA. Surely not?

TUZENBAKH. What, leaving on a name-day?

MASHA. It's all right. I'll come back this evening. Goodbye, my dear . . . (*Embraces* IRINA.) Once again, I wish you health and happiness . . . You know, in the old days, when father was alive, and it was someone's name-day, we'd have as many as thirty or forty officers arriving, and the noise . . . Today we can barely scrape up two people, and it's so quiet, it's like a desert. I'll go now. I'm in a foul mood today, I feel depressed – you don't want to listen to me. (*Laughs tearfully.*) We'll have a talk later, but I'll say goodbye now, my dear, I must go.

IRINA (*displeased*). Well, really . . .

OLGA (*in tears*). I understand you, Masha.

SOLIONY. Yes, when a man has a serious talk, it's either philosophy, or sophistry; but when a woman, or two women start talking – well, I couldn't care two hoots.

MASHA. What do you mean by that, you horrible, frightful man?

SOLIONY. Nothing. 'Before he had time to gasp, the bear had him in its grasp . . . '

A pause.

MASHA (*to* OLGA, *angrily*). Stop howling!

ANFISA *and* FERAPONT *enter, carrying a cake.*

ANFISA. In here, old man. Go on, your feet are clean enough. (*To* IRINA.) It's from the council, from Protopopov . . . he's sent a cake.

IRINA. Thank you. Tell him thanks very much.

She accepts the cake.

FERAPONT. What's that?

IRINA (*louder*). Tell him thank you!

OLGA. Nanny, give him some of the cake. Ferapont, off you go, they'll give you some cake.

FERAPONT. What?

ANFISA. Come on, old man. Ferapont, this way . . . (*Exits with* FERAPONT)

MASHA. I can't stand that Protopopov, that Mikhail Potapych or Ivanych or whatever his name is. You shouldn't invite him.

IRINA. I haven't invited him.

MASHA. Just as well.

Enter CHEBUTYKIN, *and behind him a soldier carrying a silver samovar; cries of astonishment and dismay.*

OLGA (*covering her face with her hands*). A samovar! This is terrible! (*Exits to the ballroom, by the table.*)

IRINA. Dearest Ivan Romanych, what are you doing!

TUZENBAKH (*laughs*). I told you!

MASHA. Ivan Romanych, you've absolutely no shame!

CHEBUTYKIN. My darling girls, my sweet girls, you're all I have, you're the dearest thing on earth to me. I'll be sixty soon, I'm an old man, a lonely, useless old man. There's nothing any good about me, except the love I have for you, and if it wasn't for you, well, I'd have been dead long ago . . . (*To* IRINA.) My sweet, darling child, I've known you since the day you were born . . . I've carried you in my arms . . . I loved your poor mother . . .

IRINA. But why give me such expensive presents?

CHEBUTYKIN (*through tears, angrily*). Expensive presents? Get away with you . . . (*To his batman.*) Take the samovar in there . . . (*Mimicking* IRINA.) Expensive presents . . .

The batman removes the samovar into the ballroom.

ANFISA (*passing through the drawing room*). Oh, my dears, there's a stranger arrived, a colonel! He's already taken his coat off, my dears, and he's coming in. Now, Irina, love, you be nice to him, won't you, and polite . . . (*Exits.*) And it's long past lunch-time . . . Heavens!

TUZENBAKH. That'll be Vershinin.

VERSHININ *enters.*

Lieutenant-Colonel Vershinin!

VERSHININ (*to* MASHA *and* IRINA). Allow me to introduce myself – Vershinin. I'm so pleased to be here – at last. My, how you've grown!

IRINA. Please sit down. You're very welcome.

VERSHININ (*delightedly*). I'm so glad, I really am! But surely there should be three sisters. Three little girls, I remember. I don't remember your faces, but I certainly recall your father, Colonel Prozorov, having three little girls, I remember seeing them for sure. My, doesn't time fly! Yes, time flies all right!

TUZENBAKH. Aleksandr Ignatyevich is from Moscow.

IRINA. From Moscow? You're from Moscow?

VERSHININ. Yes, I am. Your late father was battery commander there, and I was an officer in the same brigade. (*To* MASHA.) You know, I believe I do remember you, slightly.

MASHA. Well, I don't remember you!

IRINA. Olya! Olya! (*Calls into the ballroom.*) Olya, do come!

OLGA *emerges into the drawing-room.*

Lieutenant-Colonel Vershinin is from Moscow, would you believe.

VERSHININ. You must be the older sister, Olga Serge-yevna . . . And you're Mariya . . . And you're Irina – the youngest . . .

OLGA. You're from Moscow?

VERSHININ. Yes. I studied in Moscow, entered the service in Moscow – served there a long time, until I eventually got this battery – transferred here, as you see. I don't remember you in detail, only that you were three sisters. Your father's stayed in my memory, though. I need only close my eyes and I can see him, as large as life. I used to visit you in Moscow.

OLGA. I thought I could remember everybody, but now . . .

VERSHININ. I'm Aleksandr Ignatyevich . . .

IRINA. Aleksandr Ignatyevich, and you're from Moscow . . . That really is amazing!

OLGA. We'll be moving there, you see.

IRINA. Yes, we should be there by autumn, we think. It's our home town, we were born there . . . On Old Basmanny Street . . .

They both laugh delightedly.

MASHA. They've spotted a fellow-Muscovite. (*animatedly.*) Ah, now I remember! Olya, you remember all the talk about the 'lovesick Major' . . . You were a lieutenant then, and you were in love with somebody or other, and they all used to tease you, calling you a major for some reason . . .

VERSHININ (*laughs*). That's right, that's right . . . 'The lovesick Major', it's true . . .

MASHA. You only had a moustache then . . . Oh, and you've got so much older! (*Tearfully.*) You've grown so old!

VERSHININ. Yes, when they called me the lovesick Major, I was still young, and in love. And now I'm not.

OLGA. But you haven't a single grey hair. You've grown older, yes, but you're not old.

VERSHININ. Well, I don't know, I've turned forty-two. Have you been away from Moscow long?

IRINA. Eleven years. Masha, you're crying, what's wrong? Don't be silly . . . (*Tearfully.*) Now I'll start crying . . .

MASHA. I'm all right. Where did you stay in Moscow?

VERSHININ. On Old Basmanny Street.

OLGA. Why, so did we . . ,

VERSHININ. At one time I stayed in Nemetsky Street, and I used to walk from Nemetsky Street to the Krasny Barracks. There's a gloomy-looking bridge on the way, with the water roaring underneath it. You could feel quite depressed, if you were on your own.

A pause.

Still, the river here's so wide, so majestic! A superb river!

OLGA. Yes, but it's cold. It's cold here, and the mosquitoes . . .

VERSHININ. Nonsense! It's fine and healthy, a good Russian climate. The forest, the river . . . you've got birch-trees too. The gentle, modest birch, I love it above all other trees. It's a good life here. The only odd thing is the railway station, fifteen miles away . . . And nobody seems to know why.

SOLIONY. Well, I know why.

Everyone turns to look at him.

It's because if the station were nearer, then it wouldn't be so far, but since it's far, that means it isn't near.

An awkward silence.

TUZENBAKH. You're a great joker, Soliony.

OLGA. Now I've remembered you too. I do remember.

VERSHININ. I knew your dear mother.

CHEBUTYKIN. She was a fine woman, may God rest her soul.

IRINA. Mama was buried in Moscow.

OLGA. In the Novo-Devichy cemetery . . .

MASHA. Would you believe, I'm already beginning to forget her face? We won't be remembered either. We'll be forgotten.

VERSHININ. Forgotten, yes. That's our fate, and there's nothing we can do about it. What seems so important or significant to us, what we take so seriously, well, in time it'll all be forgotten, or else seem trivial.

A pause.

And the strange thing is, we can have absolutely no idea
what people will come to value, or think important, and
what they'll find pathetic or ludicrous. I mean, didn't the
discoveries of Copernicus, or Columbus, say, seem
pointless and stupid at first, while the most arrant nonsense, scribbled down by some crank, passed for truth? It
could even be that this life of ours, which we take so much
for granted, will come to be seen as bizarre and uncomfortable, mindless, and none too clean, maybe even sinful . . .

TUZENBAKH. Who knows? It's also possible that our life
will be highly thought of, and people will look back on it
with respect. We don't have torture nowadays, or
executions, or invasions, though there's still a great deal of
suffering!

SOLIONY (*in a squeaky voice*). Cheep! Cheep! Cheep! . . . Just
give the Baron the floor, and he's as happy as a sandboy!

TUZENBAKH. Soliony, I wish you'd leave me in peace . . .
(*Sits apart.*) It's very boring, if you must know.

SOLIONY. Cheep! Cheep! Cheep!

TUZENBAKH (*to* VERSHININ). Yes, the suffering we see
around us today – and there's so much of it – even so, it
indicates a certain rise in moral standards, which our
society has already achieved . . .

VERSHININ. Yes, of course.

CHEBUTYKIN. Baron, you've just said that people'll look
up to us, but we're pretty small all the same . . . (*Stands up.*)
Look how small I am, for instance. You've obviously got to
say my life has some sort of value and meaning, just to
console me.

In the adjoining room, a violin is being played.

MASHA. That's Andrei, our brother.

IRINA. He's the brains in our family. He really ought to be a professor. Papa was a soldier, but his son's chosen an academic career.

MASHA. At Papa's wish.

OLGA. We've been teasing him today. We think he's a little in love.

IRINA. With a young lady locally. She'll be here today, very possibly.

MASHA. Ugh! The way she dresses! Not just unattractive and unfashionable – it's absolutely pitiful. Some sort of bizarre, garish yellow skirt, with a silly fringe and a red blouse. And her cheeks shining, absolutely scrubbed! No, Andrei isn't in love, I won't hear of it – he's got more taste, he's simply teasing us, playing the fool. I heard yesterday she was going to marry Protopopov, the chairman of our local council. And a good thing, too. (*Calling through the side door.*) Andrei, come here! Just for a minute, dear!

ANDREI *enters.*

OLGA. This is my brother, Andrei Sergeyich.

VERSHININ. Vershinin.

ANDREI. Prozorov. (*Wipes the perspiration from his brow.*) So, you're our new battery commander?

OLGA. Just imagine, Aleksandr Ignatych is from Moscow.

ANDREI. Really? Well, I congratulate you, my dear sisters won't give you any peace now.

VERSHININ. Oh, I've already managed to bore your sisters.

IRINA. Look at the little picture frame Andrei gave me today! (*Shows him the frame.*) He made it himself.

VERSHININ (*inspects the frame, uncertain what to say*). Yes, it's . . . it's very . . .

IRINA. And that little frame over the piano, he made that too.

ANDREI w*aves his hand dismissively and moves apart.*

OLGA. He's our intellectual as well, and he plays the violin – he makes all sorts of little things out of wood. Really, he's a jack of all trades. Andrei, don't go! Oh, that's his way, he's always running off. Andrei, come back!

MASHA *and* IRINA *take hold of his arms and lead him back, laughing.*

MASHA. Come on, come on.

ANDREI. Let me go, please.

MASHA. You're so funny! They used to call Aleksandr Ignatyevich the lovesick Major, and it didn't upset him.

VERSHININ. Not in the least!

MASHA. And I'm going to call you . . . the lovesick fiddler!

IRINA. Or the lovesick professor!

OLGA. He's in love! Andryusha's in love!

IRINA (*clapping her hands*). Bravo! Bravo! Andryusha's in love!

CHEBUTYKIN *approaches* ANDREI *from behind and seizes him with both arms around his waist.*

CHEBUTYKIN. 'For love alone did Nature bring us forth upon this Earth!' (*Laughs, still holding his newspaper.*)

ANDREI. Enough, enough! (*Mopping his brow.*) I haven't slept all night, and I'm not exactly at my best, as they say. I read till four o'clock, then went to bed, but it wasn't any use. I kept thinking, about this and that, but the dawn comes up early here, and next thing the sun's creeping into my bedroom. While I'm here I want to spend the summer translating a little book from English.

VERSHININ. You read English?

ANDREI. Oh yes, our father, God bless him, burdened us with an education. It's a ludicrous idea, I know, but I must confess I've started to put on weight since his death, and I've got quite stout in a year, as you see, as if my body's been relieved of its burden. Thanks to father, my sisters and I know French, German and English, and Irina also knows Italian. But at what cost!

MASHA. In this town, knowing three languages is an unnecessary luxury. No, not even a luxury – a useless appendage, like a sixth finger. Superfluous knowledge.

VERSHININ. I don't believe it! (*Laughs.*) Superfluous? I don't think there's a town anywhere – there can't be – that's so dismal and boring that it has no use for an intelligent, well-educated person. Let's say that among a population of a hundred thousand in this town, backward and ignorant, agreed – let's say there are only three like yourselves. It stands to reason you can't win over the benighted masses all around you; in the course of your life, little by little, you'll be forced to submit, lose yourself in the crowd, the hundred thousand. Life'll swallow you up, but you won't disappear all the same, you won't cease to have some influence; after you've gone, there'll be others like you, perhaps six, then twelve, and so on, until finally people like you will be in the majority. In two or three hundred years' time, life on this earth will be unimaginably beautiful, astonishing. Man needs such a life, and even if it isn't here yet, he's still got to have a presentiment of it, to wait, and dream, and prepare for it, and that's why he has to see more, know more, than his father and grandfather did. (*Laughs.*) And you're talking about superfluous knowledge!

MASHA (*takes off her hat*). I'll stay for lunch.

IRINA (*with a sigh*). We really ought to have noted all that down . . .

ANDREI *has slipped out, unnoticed.*

TUZENBAKH. What you're saying is that after many years, life on earth'll be beautiful and astonishing. That's true. But in order to be a part of it now, remote as we may be, we must prepare ourselves for it, we must work . . .

VERSHININ (*rises*). Yes. Still, what a lot of flowers you have! (*Looking round.*) And such a splendid house. I envy you! I've knocked around all my life in poky rooms, with two chairs and a sofa, and stoves forever belching smoke. Yes, there's been a distinct shortage of flowers like this in my life! (*Rubs his hands together.*) Ah, well, never mind, eh?

TUZENBAKH. Yes, we must work. No doubt you're thinking, well, that's just a German getting emotional. But

I'm Russian, my word of honour – I don't even speak German. My father's Orthodox . . .

A pause.

VERSHININ (*pacing about the stage*). You know, I often think: what if we could start life over again, knowing what we do now? If this one life, which we've lived out, could've been a rough draft, as they say, and the next one, the fair copy! Well, first and foremost, my guess is we'd try not to repeat ourselves. At the very least we'd create a different set of circumstances for ourselves, a house like this, say, with flowers, flooded with light . . . I have a wife, and two little girls, and on top of that, my lady wife doesn't keep well, and so forth. But if I could begin life over again, I wouldn't get married . . . No, indeed!

KULYGIN *enters, in his uniform frock coat.*

KULYGIN (*goes up to* IRINA). My dear sister, allow me to congratulate you on your saint's day, and to wish you, most sincerely, from the bottom of my heart, good health, and everything a young woman of your age could hope for. And also to make you a present of this little book. (*Hands her the book.*) It's the history of our school during the last fifty years, written by myself. It's a trifling thing, written to pass the time, but do read it all the same. Good morning, ladies and gentlemen! (*To* VERSHININ.) I'm Kulygin, teacher at the local high school, and court counsellor. (*To* IRINA.) You'll find the names in there of everyone who passed through our school in the last fifty years. *Feci quod potui, faciant meliora potentes.* (*He kisses* MASHA.)

IRINA. But you already gave me this book, at Easter.

KULYGIN (*laughs*). No, it's not possible! Well, in that case give it back to me – or better still, give it to the Colonel. Please take it, Colonel. You can read it sometime when you've nothing better to do.

VERSHININ. Thank you. (*Makes ready to leave.*) Well, I'm extremely pleased to have made your acquaintance . . .

OLGA. You're leaving? Surely not!

IRINA. Stay and have lunch with us. Please.

OLGA. Yes, please stay.

VERSHININ (*bows*). I seem to have intruded on a name day party. Forgive me, I didn't know, and I haven't congratulated you . . . (*Exits with* OLGA *to the ballroom.*)

KULYGIN. Ladies and gentlemen, today is Sunday, a day of rest, and rest we shall. We shall amuse ourselves, each one as befits his age and condition. These carpets'll have to be taken up for the summer, and put away until winter . . . they'll need some Persian powder, or naphthalene . . . Yes, the Romans were healthy, because they knew how to work, and how to rest, they had *mens sana in corpore sano*. Their lives had a distinct form. As our headmaster says, the most important thing about any sort of life is its form . . . Anything that loses its form is finished – and it's exactly the same with our everyday lives. (*He clasps* MASHA *around the waist, laughing.*) Masha loves me. My wife loves me. Yes, and the curtains should be put away along with the carpets . . . Today I'm happy, I'm in excellent high spirits. Masha, we have to be at the headmaster's today at four o'clock. He's organised a little outing for the teachers and their families.

MASHA. I'm not going.

KULYGIN (*pained*). But, Masha dear, why not?

MASHA. We'll talk about it later . . . (*Crossly.*) Oh, all right, I'll go. Just leave me alone, please. (*She moves apart.*)

KULYGIN. And afterwards we're to spend the evening at the headmaster's house. You know, in spite of ill health, that man does his level best to be sociable. A first-rate individual, quite brilliant – a truly magnificent man. After the staff meeting yesterday, he said to me, 'I'm tired, Fyodor! I'm so tired!' (*Looks at the wall-clock, then at his watch.*) Your clock's seven minutes fast. 'Yes,' he says, 'I'm tired.'

A violin is being played off-stage.

OLGA. Gentlemen, please sit down to lunch! It's a pie!

KULYGIN. Ah, my dear Olga, dear kind Olga! I had to work all day yesterday, from morning till eleven o'clock at night, I'm tired, and today I feel so happy. (*Exits to the table in the ballroom.*) My dearest Olga!

CHEBUTYKIN (*puts his newspaper into his pocket, and strokes his beard*). A pie? Wonderful!

MASHA (*to CHEBUTYKIN, severely*). Just see you don't drink today. Do you hear? Drinking's bad for you.

CHEBUTYKIN. Oh, stuff – I've got over all that. It's two years since I last hit the bottle. (*Testily.*) Anyway, what difference does it make?

MASHA. You'd better not, all the same. Don't you dare drink! (*Angrily, but taking care her husband doesn't hear.*) Damn! Another whole evening, bored stiff at the headmaster's!

TUZENBAKH. If I were you, I wouldn't go . . . Simple as that.

CHEBUTYKIN. Don't go, my dear.

MASHA. Oh yes, don't go . . . This damnable life, I can't bear it . . . (*Exits to the ballroom.*)

CHEBUTYKIN (*exits behind her*). Well, well . . .

SOLIONY (*as he crosses to the ballroom*). Cheep! Cheep! Cheep!

TUZENBAKH. That's enough, Soliony. Give it a rest.

SOLIONY. Cheep! Cheep! Cheep!

KULYGIN (*cheerfully*). Your good health, Colonel! Yes, I'm a schoolmaster, one of the family here, Masha's husband. She's a good woman, a very kind woman . . .

VERSHININ. I think I'll have some of this dark vodka . . . (*Drinks.*) Your good health! (*To* OLGA.) I feel really at home here! . . .

IRINA *and* TUZENBAKH *remain alone in the drawing room.*

IRINA. Masha's in a bad mood today. She got married at eighteen, when she thought he was the cleverest of men. Now, she doesn't. He's the kindest, but not the cleverest.

OLGA (*impatiently*). Andrei, what's keeping you!

ANDREI (*off-stage*). I'm coming! (*He enters and comes to the table.*)

TUZENBAKH. What're you thinking?

IRINA. Oh, nothing . . . You know, I don't like that Soliony of yours, he frightens me. He says such stupid things.

TUZENBAKH. He's a strange man. I feel sorry for him. He

annoys me, but more often I pity him. I think he's shy . . . When it's just the two of us, he's quite witty and charming, but in company he can be extremely rude, a real bully. No, don't go, let them get settled first. I want to stay here with you a minute. What're you thinking about?

A pause.

You're twenty, Irina, and I'm not yet thirty. And we've so many years left ahead of us, a long, long line of days, filled with my love for you . . .

IRINA. Nikolai, please don't speak to me about love.

TUZENBAKH (*not listening*). I have a desperate thirst for life, for the struggle, for work, and this thirst in my soul has merged with my love for you, Irina. It's as if by design – you're beautiful, and that's why I find life so beautiful. Tell me what you're thinking.

IRINA. You say life is beautiful. Well, yes, but supposing it only seems that way? Life hasn't been beautiful for us yet, us three sisters. It's trampled us down, like weeds . . . My eyes are filling up. I mustn't cry . . . (*Hurriedly dries her eyes, smiles.*) We must work, work! That's why we're so depressed, and have such a gloomy outlook on life – it's because we know nothing of work. We've come from people who despised work . . .

NATALYA IVANOVNA *enters, dressed in a pink frock with a green belt.*

NATASHA They're sitting down to lunch already . . . I'm late . . . (*Glances in passing at the mirror, composes herself.*) My hair's not too bad, I think. (*Catching sight of* IRINA.) Irina Sergeyevna, my dear, congratulations! (*Gives her a firm, prolonged kiss.*) You've got so many guests, I'm really embarrassed . . . Good morning, Baron!

OLGA (*entering the drawing room*). And Natasha's here now, too! How are you, my dear!

They embrace.

NATASHA. And it's Irina's name-day, congratulations! You've got such a crowd of people, I feel terribly awkward . . .

OLGA. Don't be silly, we're all family here. (*Sotto voce, alarmed.*) You're wearing a green belt. My dear, that's all wrong!

NATASHA. Is it bad luck?

OLGA. No, no, it just doesn't match . . . it's a bit odd . . .

NATASHA (*a catch in her voice*). D'you think so? Actually, it's not green, it's more sort of neutral. (*She follows* OLGA *into the ballroom.*)

They sit down to lunch in the ballroom; the drawing room is now completely deserted.

KULYGIN. I wish you a handsome young man, Irina. It's time you were getting married.

CHEBUTYKIN. And I wish you a fine young man too, Natasha!

KULYGIN. Natasha already has a young man in mind.

MASHA. Well, I shall down a little glass of wine! Yes, why not, let's eat, drink and be damned!

KULYGIN. That's a C-minus for conduct, Masha.

VERSHININ. This is a fine liqueur. What's it made from?

SOLIONY. From cockroaches.

IRINA (*close to tears*). Ugh! That's really disgusting! . . .

OLGA. For supper we're having roast turkey, and apple pie. Thank goodness I've got the whole day at home, the evening too . . . Do come this evening, gentlemen . . .

VERSHININ. Am I allowed to come too?

IRINA. By all means.

NATASHA. They don't stand on ceremony here.

CHEBUTYKIN. 'For love alone did Nature bring us forth upon this Earth . . . ' (*Laughs.*)

ANDREI (*annoyed*). Oh, stop it, all of you! Don't you ever get tired?

FEDOTIK *and* RODE *enter carrying a large basket of flowers.*

FEDOTIK. But they're already at lunch.

RODE (*loudly, with a guttural accent*). They're at lunch? Yes, so they are . . .

FEDOTIK. Hold on a minute! (*He takes a photograph.*) One! And again, wait a second . . . (*He takes another photograph.*) Two! Now we're ready!

They carry the basket into the ballroom, where they are noisily welcomed.

RODE (*shouts*). Congratulations, all the very best! The weather's wonderful today, an absolute marvel. I've been out walking with the high school boys all morning. I teach them gymnastics.

FEDOTIK. You can move now, Irina, it's all right! (*Taking a photograph.*) You look quite special today. (*Produces a spinning-top from his pocket.*) Look what I have besides – a top . . . it makes an amazing sound . . .

IRINA. What a lovely thing!

MASHA. 'By a curving shore stands a green oak tree, bound with a chain of gold . . . ' 'Bound with a chain of gold . . . ' (*Tearfully.*) Why do I keep saying that? That line's been going through my head since morning . . .

KULYGIN. Thirteen at table!

RODE (*shouts*). Gentlemen, gentlemen, you surely don't attach any significance to superstitions?

Laughter.

KULYGIN. Thirteen at table, that means there's somebody in love. It's not you by any chance, Ivan Romanych?

Laughter.

CHEBUTYKIN. No, I'm just an old sinner, but Natasha's blushing, and I can't for the life of me think why[1]

Hearty laughter. NATASHA *rushes out of the ballroom into the drawing room, pursued by* ANDREI.

ANDREI. Don't worry, don't take any notice of them! Wait, don't go, please . . .

NATASHA. I'm so ashamed . . . I don't know what's the matter with me, and they're making a fool of me. I shouldn't have left the table, it's bad manners, but I can't help it . . . I just can't . . .

Covers her face with her hands.

ANDREI. Oh, my dear love, please don't be upset. They're only joking, honestly, they're harmless. Dearest, darling Natasha, they're good people, kindhearted, and they love us both. Come over to the window, where they can't see us . . . (*He looks around.*)

NATASHA. I'm just not used to company! . . .

ANDREI. Oh, you're so young, so beautiful, so wonderful! My dear, sweet Natasha, you mustn't get upset . . . Believe me, please, trust me . . . I'm so happy, my heart's filled with love and joy . . . No, no, they can't see us, they can't! I don't know why I've fallen in love with you, or when it happened – oh, I don't know anything. My dearest, good, pure Natasha, be my wife! I love you, I love you as I've never loved anyone . . .

They kiss.

Two officers enter, and catching sight of the embracing couple, pause in astonishment.

Curtain.

Act Two

The stage is set as in Act One. It is eight o'clock in the evening. Off-stage, an accordion is being played outside, faintly audible. The room is unlit. NATASHA enters in her dressing-gown, holding a candle. She crosses the stage and pauses at the door leading to ANDREI's room.

NATASHA. Andrei, what are you doing? You're reading? Oh, it doesn't matter, I was just wondering . . . (*She moves on, opens another door, looks in, then closes it.*) No lights left on . . .

ANDREI.(*emerging with a book in his hand*). What is it, Natasha?

NATASHA. I'm checking to see if there's a light on . . . It's carnival time, the servants are getting careless, you have to keep an eye on them constantly, to make sure nothing's wrong. I walked through the dining room at midnight last night, and there was a candle left burning. And I still haven't found out who lit it. (*She sets down the candle.*) What time is it?

ANDREI (*looks at his watch*). Quarter past eight.

NATASHA. And Olga and Irina still aren't in. They haven't come home. They're kept busy the whole time, poor things. Olga at her staff meeting, Irina at her telegraph office . . . (*Sighs.*) I said that to your sister this morning, 'You must look after yourself, Irina darling,' I said. But she doesn't listen. Quarter past eight, did you say? You know, I'm afraid our little Bobik isn't at all well. Why is he so cold? He had a fever yesterday, and today he's freezing . . .

I'm really worried about him!

ANDREI. He's fine, Natasha. The boy's fine.

NATASHA. Still, we'd better see he's eating properly. I'm worried. And there's supposed to be carnival people arriving at ten o'clock, I'd rather they didn't come, Andryusha.

ANDREI. Well, I don't know . . . After all, we did invite them.

NATASHA. You know, that darling little boy woke up this morning and looked at me, and he suddenly smiled – yes, he recognised me. 'Hello, Bobik!' I said, 'Hello, my darling!' And he laughed, yes. Children know everything that's going on, they understand perfectly. Anyway, Andryusha, I'll tell them not to let the musicians in.

ANDREI (*indecisively*). Well, that's surely up to my sisters. I mean, it's their house . . .

NATASHA. Yes, of course, I'll tell them too. They're so kind . . . (*Makes to leave.*) I've ordered sour milk for supper. The doctor says you're to have nothing but sour milk, otherwise you'll never lose weight. (*Pauses.*) Bobik gets a chill so easily. I'm worried in case it's too cold for him in there. We ought to put him in another room, at least until the warm weather. Irina's room, for instance – that's just perfect for a baby: it's dry, and it gets the sun all day. She'll have to be told, and she can move in with Olga meantime . . . She's not at home during the day anyway, she's only here at nights . . .

A pause.

Andryusha, love, you're not answering.

ANDREI. I'm thinking . . . Anyway, I've nothing to say . . .

NATASHA. Well . . . There was something I meant to tell
you . . . Oh yes, Ferapont's come from the council, he
wants to see you.

ANDREI (*Yawns*). Send him in.

NATASHA *exits.* ANDREI, *stooping over the candle she has left
behind, goes on reading his book.* FERAPONT *enters; he is
wearing an old shabby overcoat, with the collar turned up, and a
scarf round his ears.*

Well, hello, old chap – what is it?

FERAPONT. The Chairman's sent you a book, and papers
of some sort. I've got them here . . . (*Hands over a book, and
a package.*)

ANDREI. Thank you. That's fine. Why didn't you come
earlier? It's gone eight o'clock.

FERAPONT. What?

ANDREI (*louder*) I said, you're late, it's eight o'clock already.

FERAPONT. That's true. It was still light when I came to see
you, but they wouldn't let me in, no. The master's busy,
they said. Well, never mind. If you're busy, you're busy,
I'm in no hurry. (*He thinks* ANDREI *has asked him something.*)
What?

ANDREI. Nothing. (*Inspects the book.*) Tomorrow's Friday,
there's no meeting, but I'll go in anyway . . . it'll give me
something to do. I'm bored stiff at home . . .

A pause.

Yes, my dear old chap, it's odd how things change, how life plays tricks on us. Out of sheer boredom today, nothing better to do, I picked up this book – my old university lectures, and I thought it was so funny . . . Good God, I'm the secretary to the district council, under chairman Protopopov – I'm secretary, and the most I can aspire to is to become a member! Yes, me – a member of the district council . . . and there I am dreaming every night that I'm a professor at Moscow University, a famous scholar, the pride of all Russia!

FERAPONT. I dunno . . . I don't hear too well . . .

ANDREI. Well, if you *could* hear, I doubt if I'd be talking like this. I've got to talk to somebody, but my wife doesn't understand me, and for some reason or other I'm afraid of my sisters. I'm afraid they'll laugh at me, or make me feel ashamed . . . I don't drink, I don't like taverns, but oh, my dear old chap, what wouldn't I give to be sitting right now in Moscow at Tyestov's, or the Grand Hotel!

FERAPONT. A builder at the council was saying just the other day that some merchants in Moscow were eating pancakes; and one of them, who'd eaten forty of the things, dropped down dead. Maybe it wasn't forty, maybe it was fifty. I don't rightly recall.

ANDREI. Yes, you can sit in Moscow, in an enormous restaurant dining-room, you don't know anybody, nobody knows you, and yet you don't feel like a stranger. But in this place, you know everybody, everybody knows you, but you're an outsider, a total stranger . . . Alone, and alien . . .

FERAPONT. What?

A pause.

That same builder was saying – maybe he was making it up – he said there was a rope stretched right across Moscow, from one end to the other.

ANDREI. What for?

FERAPONT. I dunno. That's what the builder said.

ANDREI. That's rubbish. (*Returns to his book.*) Have you ever been in Moscow?

FERAPONT (*After a pause*). I haven't. It's not been God's will.

A pause.

Shall I go?

ANDREI. You can go now. Take care, old chap.

FERAPONT *exits.*

Take care. (*Reading.*) You can come back tomorrow morning, collect these papers . . . Off you go . . .

A pause.

He's gone.

The door-bell rings.

Yes, more work . . . (*Stretches, and makes his way slowly off to his own room.*)

The old nurse is heard singing off-stage, rocking the baby to sleep. MASHA and VERSHININ enter. While they converse, a maid lights the oil-lamp and candles.

MASHA. I don't know.

A pause.

I don't know. Habit counts for a great deal, of course, what you're accustomed to. After father's death, for example, we just couldn't get used to the fact that we didn't have orderlies any longer. But quite apart from habit, I think I'm justified in saying this. Maybe it isn't the same in other places, but in this town the most decent, the most honourable and well-bred people are the military.

VERSHININ. I'm really thirsty. I wouldn't mind some tea.

MASHA (*glancing at her watch*). They'll be bringing it soon. Yes, I got married when I was eighteen – I was in awe of my husband, because he was a teacher, and I'd only just left school. He was terribly learned, clever and important, so I thought. And now I don't, sad to say.

VERSHININ. Yes . . . I see.

MASHA. I'm not talking about my husband, I've got used to him, but among civilians in general there are so many boorish people, no manners, badly brought up. It upsets me, rudeness really offends me – when people show a lack of sensitivity, or kindness, or common courtesy, I feel pain. When I'm with the teachers, for instance, my husband's colleagues, I really suffer.

VERSHININ. Yes . . . Even so, I think the military and civilians are pretty much of a muchness, in this town at any rate. No difference! If you listen to any educated person hereabouts, soldier or civilian, they're fed up with their wives, they're fed up with their house or their land, they're sick to death of their horses . . . I mean, why is it that

Russians, who lay claim to the most exalted ideas, have such low expectations of life? Why is that?

MASHA. Why?

VERSHININ. Why is your average Russian sick to death of his wife and children? And why are his wife and children sick of him?

MASHA. You're not at your best today.

VERSHININ. It's possible. I haven't eaten today, I've had nothing since morning. My daughter's a bit off-colour, and whenever my little girls are ill I get terribly worried, I get conscience-stricken about the sort of mother they have. Oh, you should have seen her today! Talk about pettyminded! We started shouting at each other at seven in the morning, and at nine I slammed the door and left.

A pause.

I never talk about these things, and it's strange I should be telling you. (*He kisses her hand.*) Don't be angry with me. Apart from you, I have nobody, no-one at all . . .

A pause

MASHA. The stove's making such a noise. The chimney howled like that just before Father died. Exactly like that.

VERSHININ. You're not superstitious?

MASHA. Yes.

VERSHININ. That's odd. (*He kisses her hand.*) What a magnificent, wonderful creature you are. Truly magnificent, and wonderful! It's dark in here, yet I can still see your eyes shining.

MASHA (*sits down on another chair*). It's lighter over here . . .

VERSHININ. I love you, I love you . . . I love your eyes, your every movement, I dream about them . . . A magnificent, wonderful woman!

MASHA (*softly laughing*). When you speak to me like that, I laugh, I don't know why, even though I'm terrified. Please, don't say it again . . . (*Barely audible.*) No, go on, say it, I don't mind . . . (*Covers her face with her hands.*) It doesn't matter. There's someone coming, change the subject . . .

IRINA *and* TUZENBAKH *enter through the ballroom.*

TUZENBAKH. Yes, I have a triple-barrelled name – Baron Tuzenbakh-Krone-Altschauer, but I'm Russian, and Orthodox, the same as you. There's hardly any of the German left in me, unless you count my dogged persistence, the way I keep pestering you, walking you home every evening.

IRINA. Oh, I'm worn out!

TUZENBAKH. And I'll turn up at the telegraph office every day and walk you home, I'll do that for ten, twenty years, until you chase me away . . . (*Catches sight of* MASHA *and* VERSHININ, *delightedly.*) Oh, it's you! Hello!

IRINA. Home at last! (*To* MASHA.) You know, a woman came in just now, she was sending a telegram to her brother in Saratov, to let him know her son had died, and she couldn't for the life of her remember his address. And she sent it off like that, without an address, just Saratov. She was crying, and I was rude to her for no good reason. 'I haven't got all day,' I said. It was really stupid of me. Are we having the musicians tonight?

MASHA. Yes.

IRINA (*sits in the armchair*). I need a rest. I'm exhausted.

TUZENBAKH (*smiling*). Every time you come in from work
you look such a pathetic little thing . . .

A pause.

IRINA. I'm tired. No, I don't like that telegraph office, I
really don't.

MASHA. You've got thinner . . . (*Whistles.*) And younger-
looking, quite boyish about the face . . .

TUZENBAKH. That's her hair-style.

IRINA. I'll have to find another job, this isn't for me.
Whatever I wanted so much, and dreamed about, this
definitely isn't it. There's no poetry in the work, it's
mindless . . .

A knocking on the floor.

That's the Doctor knocking. (*To* TUZENBAKH.) Be a
dear and answer him . . . I can't . . . I'm too tired . . .

TUZENBAKH *knocks on the floor.*

He'll be up any minute. We'll have to do something about
this. He was with Andrei at the club yesterday, losing
money again. Andrei lost two hundred roubles, apparently.

MASHA (*indifferently*). There's nothing we can do about that.

IRINA. He lost money a fortnight ago, and in December,
too. I wish he'd lose everything, then perhaps we'd be
able to get away from this town. Dear God in Heaven,
I dream about Moscow every night, it's as if I'm going

crazy. (*Laughs.*) We'll be moving there in June, and between now and June there's still . . . February, March, April . . . May . . . almost six months!

MASHA. Let's just hope Natasha doesn't find out about the money he's lost.

IRINA. I don't think she cares.

CHEBUTYKIN *has just got up out of bed, an after-dinner nap, and he now enters the ballroom, stroking his beard, sits down at the table and takes a newspaper out of his pocket.*

MASHA. Here he is now . . . Has he paid his rent?

IRINA (*laughs*). No. Not a penny for the past eight months. It's obviously slipped his mind.

MASHA (*laughs*). And sitting there, so self-importantly!

They all laugh. A pause.

IRINA. You're very quiet, Colonel?

VERSHININ. Yes, I don't know why. I'd like some tea. My kingdom for a glass of tea! I've had nothing to eat since morning . . .

CHEBUTYKIN. Irina Sergeyevna . . .

IRINA. Yes, what is it?

CHEBUTYKIN. Come here, please. *Venez ici*!

IRINA *goes to him and sits down at the table.*

I need your help.

IRINA *begins setting out the cards for a game of patience.*

VERSHININ. Oh well, if they won't give us any tea, then at least we can have a discussion.

TUZENBAKH. Yes, let's – what about?

VERSHININ. What about? Well, let's imagine, for example, what life'll be like after we're gone, say in two, or three hundred years' time.

TUZENBAKH. Really? Well, people'll fly around in balloons, there'll be a new fashion in men's jackets, they'll possibly discover some sixth sense, and develop it, but basically life'll remain the same – difficult, full of mystery, and happy. Yes, in a thousand years' time people'll still be sighing: 'God, what a life!' – and they'll be just as afraid of death, just as unwilling to die, as they are now.

VERSHININ (*after some thought*). I'm not sure, but it seems to me that everything in life changes, little by little, it must do, and it's already happening, before our very eyes. In two or three hundred years' time, or a thousand, say – it doesn't matter how long – a new, happy life will dawn. Of course, we shan't be a part of that life, but we're living and working towards it now, suffering, indeed, to create it, and that's the whole point of our existence, that's our happiness, if you like.

MASHA *laughs softly.*

TUZENBAKH. What is it?

MASHA. Oh, nothing. I've been laughing the whole day.

VERSHININ. Well, I went to the same cadet school as you, I didn't go on to the Academy. I read a great deal, but I've no idea how to choose books, and possibly I don't read the things I should, but the longer I live, the more I want to know. My hair's turning grey, I'm practically an old man, and yet I understand so little – so very little. Nevertheless, I think I know what's genuinely important – yes, that I do know. I just wish I could prove to you that there's no such thing as happiness, there simply can't be, for us . . . All we can do is keep working, but as for happiness – well, that's reserved for our remote descendants.

A pause.

Not for me, no, but at least posterity, my children's children.

FEDOTIK *and* RODE *appear in the ballroom; they sit down and begin quietly singing, to a guitar accompaniment.*

TUZENBAKH. So, according to you, we can't even imagine happiness. But what if I'm happy now?

VERSHININ. You aren't.

TUZENBAKH (*throws up his hands, laughing*). Well, obviously we don't understand each other. So, how am I to convince you?

MASHA *laughs softly.*

(*Wags his finger at her.*) Go ahead and laugh. (*To* VERSHININ.) Yes, whether it's two, or three hundred years, or even a million years from now, life'll be the same as it's always been; it doesn't change, it remains constant, following its own laws, which don't concern us, or at least we can never know. Take migrating birds, for instance, like cranes – they keep on flying, and no matter what kind of thoughts, great or small, should pass through their heads, they'll fly on and on just the same, without knowing why or where to. They fly, and they'll keep flying, supposing all manner of thinkers were to spring up amongst them. They can think all they want, as long as they keep flying . . .

VERSHININ. And what about meaning?

TUZENBAKH. Meaning? . . . Look, it's snowing. What does that mean?

A pause.

MASHA. I think people should believe in something, or seek after truth, otherwise their lives are empty, just empty . . . To live, without knowing why cranes fly, or why children are born, or why there are stars in the sky . . . I mean, you either know why you're alive, or else it's all just nonsense, absolutely pointless . . .

A pause.

VERSHININ. Still, it's a shame we're no longer young.

MASHA. As Gogol says, 'Life's a bore, my friends!'

TUZENBAKH. Yes, and I say it's hard work arguing with you, my friends! I give up . . .

CHEBUTYKIN (*reading from his newspaper*). Balzac got married in Berdichev.

IRINA *begins softly singing.*

I really must make a note of that. (*Notes it down.*) Balzac was married in Berdichev . . . (*Goes on reading his newspaper.*)

IRINA (*laying out a game of patience, abstractedly*). Balzac was married in Berdichev . . .

TUZENBAKH. Anyway, the die is cast. You know I'm leaving the service, Mariya Sergeyevna?

MASHA. So I've heard. I can't see anything good about that. I don't like civilians.

TUZENBAKH. Well, it can't be helped . . . (*Stands up.*) I'm not good-looking, what sort of officer do I make? Anyway, it doesn't matter . . . I'm going to work. Just as long as I can work even one day in my life, come home at night and collapse onto the bed exhausted, fall asleep on the spot. (*Exiting to the ballroom.*) Yes, working people sleep soundly, I should imagine.

FEDOTIK (*to* IRINA). Look, I bought you some coloured pencils in a shop on Moscow Street. And you can have this penknife . . .

IRINA. You've got so used to treating me like a child, but I'm a grown woman . . . (*Accepts the pencils and penknife, delightedly.*) Oh, these are lovely!

FEDOTIK. I bought myself a knife, too . . . see, have a look. There's one blade, there's another, this one's for cleaning out your ears, and this one's for your fingernails . . .

RODE (*loudly*). Doctor, how old are you?

CHEBUTYKIN. Me? Thirty-two.

Laughter.

FEDOTIK. Here, I'll show you a different kind of patience : . . (*Sets out the cards for patience.*)

The samovar is brought in. ANFISA *attends to the samovar, and after a while* NATASHA *enters and also busies herself at the table.*

SOLIONY *then arrives, greets everyone and sits down at the table.*

VERSHININ. Just listen to that wind!

MASHA. Yes. I'm sick of winter. I've already forgotten what summer's like.

IRINA. This patience is coming out, I can see it. We'll be going to Moscow.

FEDOTIK. No, it isn't. Look, the eight's covering the two of spades. (*Laughs.*) That means you won't be going to Moscow.

CHEBUTYKIN (*reading from his newspaper*). Tsitsikar . . . There's a smallpox epidemic in Tsitsikar . . .

ANFISA (*goes up to* MASHA). Masha, come and have some tea, my dear. (*To* VERSHININ.) And you too, Your Honour – I beg your pardon, sir, I've forgotten your name . . .

MASHA. Bring it here, Nanny. I'm not coming over there.

IRINA. Nanny!

ANFISA I'm coming, I'm coming.

NATASHA (*to* SOLIONY.) You know, babies really do understand. 'Hello, Bobik,' I say, 'Hello, my darling!' And he looks up at me in that special way. I mean, you think that's just a mother talking, but it isn't, I do assure you. He really is an extraordinary child.

SOLIONY. Yes, well, if that child was mine, I'd fry him up in a pan and eat him. (*Walks off, glass in hand, into the drawing-room and sits in a corner.*)

NATASHA (*covering her face with her hands*). Oh, what a rude, ignorant man!

MASHA. Some people don't even notice whether it's winter or summer. They're lucky. If I were in Moscow, I don't think I'd care twopence about the weather.

VERSHININ. I was reading a diary recently, written by some French government Minister in prison. He was jailed in connection with that business in Panama. He goes into absolute raptures about the birds he can see from his cell-window, which he'd never even noticed when he was a Minister. And of course now he's been released, he doesn't notice the birds any more. You won't notice Moscow either, once you're living there. No, there's no happiness for us, and never can be – it's just wishful thinking.

TUZENBAKH (*picks up a box from the table*). Where've all the sweets gone?

IRINA. Soliony's eaten them.

TUZENBAKH. All of them?

ANFISA (*serving the tea*). There's a message for you, sir.

VERSHININ. For me? (*Takes the note.*) It's from my daughter. (*Reads it.*) Ah, I see . . . I'm sorry, Masha, I've got to leave. I won't take any tea. (*Stands up, agitated.*) The same old story . . .

MASHA. What's wrong? If it isn't a secret?

VERSHININ (*in a low voice*). My wife's taken poison again. I must go. I'll try and slip out unnoticed. This is all dread-fully unpleasant. (*Kisses MASHA's hand.*) Oh, my dearest darling, glorious Masha . . . I'll go out this way . . . (*Exits.*)

ANFISA. Where's he gone? I've just brought his tea . . . Well, there's a fine thing.

MASHA (*flaring up*). Oh, get away! Stop pestering me, leave me in peace . . . (*She takes her cup to the table.*) You're getting on my nerves, you silly old woman!

ANFISA. Why are you so angry? Masha, my dear . . .

ANDREI *calls, off-stage: 'Anfisa!'*

ANFISA. (*mimicking*). Anfisa! And he's just sitting there . . . (*Exits.*)

MASHA (*at the table in the ballroom, angrily*). Move over, let me sit down! (*Muddles up the cards on the table.*) You've got cards spread out everywhere. Drink your tea!

IRINA. You're in a foul mood, Masha.

MASHA. Yes, well, if I'm in a foul mood, don't speak to me. Don't come near me!

CHEBUTYKIN (*laughing*). Keep off, don't touch!

MASHA. And you're sixty years of age, jabbering on like a schoolboy, a lot of damned nonsense!

NATASHA (*sighs*). Masha, my dear . . . You shouldn't use such expressions, you really shouldn't . . . I mean, with your good looks you could be quite enchanting, honestly, even in the very best society, if it weren't for your language. *Je vous prie pardonnez-moi, Marie, mais vous avez des manières un peu grossières.*

TUZENBAKH (*trying not to laugh*). Pass me that . . . pass me . . . I think that's the brandy . . .

NATASHA. *Il paraît que mon Bobik déjà ne dort pas*, he's wakened up. I don't think he's well today. I'll take a look at him, excuse me . . . (*Exits.*)

IRINA. So, where's the Colonel gone?

MASHA. Home. His wife's up to her tricks again.

TUZENBAKH (*goes up to* SOLIONY, *taking the decanter of brandy*). You're always on your own, deep in thought – and nobody knows what about, eh? Well, come on, let's be friends. Let's have some brandy.

They drink.

I'll most likely have to play the piano the whole night, all kinds of silly nonsense . . . well, that's life.

SOLIONY. Why shouldn't we be friends? I've no quarrel with you.

TUZENBAKH. No, but you always make me feel as if something's happened between us. You're a strange man, you must admit.

SOLIONY (*declaiming*). 'I am strange, yet who is not! Be not angry, Aleko!'

TUZENBAKH. What's Aleko got to do with it?

A pause.

SOLIONY. When I'm alone with someone, it's fine, I'm just like anybody else, but in company I get depressed, and withdrawn . . . I say all kinds of stupid things. Still, I'm as decent and honourable as the next man, a great deal more so, indeed. And I can prove it.

TUZENBAKH. You know, I often get angry with you, you're forever picking on me in front of people. All the same I can't help liking you. Well, so be it, I'm getting drunk tonight. Cheers!

SOLIONY. Cheers.

They drink.

I've nothing against you personally, Baron. It's just my temperament, like Lermontov's. (*Quietly.*) I even look a bit like Lermontov . . . so I've been told . . . (*He takes a bottle of scent from his pocket and pours it over his hands.*)

TUZENBAKH. Well, I shall be leaving the service. Enough! I've been thinking about it for five years, and I've finally made up my mind. I intend to work!

SOLIONY (*declaiming*). 'Be not angry, Aleko . . . Forget, forget thy dreams . . . '

While they are talking, ANDREI *enters quietly with a book, and sits down by a candle.*

TUZENBAKH. Yes, I'm going to work . . .

CHEBUTYKIN (*entering the drawing-room with* IRINA). And the food they served up was genuine Caucasian, too: onion soup, then *chekhartmá* for the meat course . . .

SOLIONY. *Cheremshá* isn't a meat dish at all, it's a vegetable, like our onion.

CHEBUTYKIN. No, no, my dear chap – *chekhartmá* isn't an onion, it's roast mutton.

SOLIONY. And I say *cheremshá* is an onion.

CHEBUTYKIN. *Chekhartmá* is mutton, I tell you.

SOLIONY. And I'm telling you – *cheremshá* is an onion!

CHEBUTYKIN. Why am I arguing with you? You've never even been to the Caucasus, you've never eaten *chekhartmá*.

SOLIONY. I've never eaten it because I can't stand it. It smells like garlic.

ANDREI (*pleading*). Gentlemen, please! Stop it!

TUZENBAKH. When are the carnival people coming?

IRINA. They said they'd be here by nine. Any minute now.

TUZENBAKH hugs ANDREI, and begins singing a comic song. ANDREI joins in, then he and CHEBUTYKIN sing and dance together, to everyone's amusement.

TUZENBAKH (*kisses ANDREI*). Damn it, let's have a drink, Andryusha, let's drink to friendship. I'm coming with you, old chap, to Moscow, to the university.

SOLIONY. Which one? There are two universities in Moscow.

ANDREI. There's only one university in Moscow.

SOLIONY. And I say there are two.

ANDREI. Why not three? The more the merrier.

SOLIONY. There are two universities in Moscow!

Murmurs of disagreement, and hissing.

There are two universities in Moscow, the old one and the new one. But if you don't care to listen to me, if my conversation annoys you, I won't speak at all. I can always go into the other room . . . (*Exits by one of the doors.*)

TUZENBAKH. Bravo, bravo! (*Laughs.*) Ladies and gentlemen, let the dancing begin, I shall sit down to play! That Soliony's so funny . . . (*Sits at the piano, begins playing a waltz.*)

MASHA (*waltzing by herself, sings*). 'The Baron's drunk, the Baron's drunk, the Baron's drunk . . . !'

Enter NATASHA.

NATASHA (*to* CHEBUTYKIN). Ivan Romanych! (*Says something to* CHEBUTYKIN, *then quietly exits.*)

CHEBUTYKIN *taps* TUZENBAKH *on the shoulder and whispers something to him.*

IRINA. What's the matter?

CHEBUTYKIN. It's time we were going. Good night, all.

TUZENBAKH. Good night. Time to go.

IRINA. What do you mean? What about the musicians?

ANDREI (*embarrassed*) There won't be any. The thing is, my dear – you see, Natasha says Bobik's not too well, and because of that . . . Oh, I don't know – frankly, I don't care either way.

IRINA (*shrugs*). Bobik's not well . . .

MASHA. Oh, to hell with it! We're being thrown out, it seems, we've got to go. (*To* IRINA.) It's not Bobik that's sick, it's her . . . Up here! (*Taps her forehead.*) Stupid woman!

ANDREI *exits right, to his own room.* CHEBUTYKIN *follows him out, the others say goodbye.*

FEDOTIK. What a shame! I'd been looking forward to spending the evening here, but if the child's sick, well, of course . . . I'll bring him a toy tomorrow . . .

RODE (*loudly*). And I had a nap after lunch today specially, I thought I'd be dancing the whole night. I mean, it's only just nine o'clock!

MASHA. Let's go outside, we can talk there. We'll decide what to do.

Cries of 'Goodbye!', 'All the best!', etc. TUZENBAKH's *merry laughter is heard, as everyone leaves.* ANFISA *and the* MAID *then clear the table, extinguish the lights, the old nurse singing as she does so.* ANDREI, *in his hat and coat, quietly enters with* CHEBUTYKIN.

CHEBUTYKIN. No, I never got round to marrying, life flashed past me like lightning. Besides, I was madly in love with your dear mother, and she was already married . . .

ANDREI. People shouldn't marry. They shouldn't, it's too boring.

CHEBUTYKIN. Ah yes, but what about loneliness? You can dress it up any way you like, my dear chap, but loneliness is a terrible thing . . . Although when all's said and done . . . well, does it really matter?

ANDREI. Let's be on our way.

CHEBUTYKIN. What's the hurry? We've plenty of time.

ANDREI. I don't want my wife stopping us.

CHEBUTYKIN. Ah, I see.

ANDREI. I won't play cards tonight, I'll just sit and watch.

I'm not feeling too well . . . What should I do about shortness of breath, d'you think?

CHEBUTYKIN. Why ask me? I can't remember, dear boy, haven't a clue!

The doorbell rings, then again. Voices are heard, laughter.

ANDREI. We'll go out through the kitchen. (*They exit.*)

IRINA (*enters*). Who is it?

ANFISA (*in a whisper*). It's the people from the carnival. (*Another ring.*)

IRINA. Nanny, tell them there's no-one home. Say we're sorry.

ANFISA *exits.* IRINA *paces about the room, deep in thought, clearly upset.* SOLIONY *enters.*

SOLIONY (*puzzled*). There's no-one here . . . Where's everyone gone?

IRINA. They've gone home.

SOLIONY. That's strange. And you're here alone?

IRINA. Yes.

A pause.

Goodnight.

SOLIONY. I behaved a little indiscreetly just now, a little tactlessly. But you're not like the others. You're high above them, you're pure, you can see the truth . . . You're the only one who understands me. I love you, with a deep, everlasting . . .

IRINA. Goodnight! Please leave.

SOLIONY. I can't live without you (*Following her.*) You're my soul's delight, my happiness! (*Through tears.*) Your wonderful, dazzling, astonishing eyes, like no other woman's I've ever seen | . .

IRINA (*coldly*). Captain Soliony, stop it.

SOLIONY. This is the first time I've spoken of my love for you, and it's as if I were on another planet, not on this earth. (*Rubs his forehead.*) Well, all right, it doesn't matter. Obviously I can't force you to love me | . . . But I won't tolerate a successful rival | . . . I won't | . . I swear to you, by all that's holy, I'll kill any rival | . . Oh, you wonderful creature . . | .

NATASHA *crosses the room with a candle.*

NATASHA (*looks into one room, then another, and walks past the door leading to her husband's room*). Andrei'll be in there. Reading, I suppose. Oh, I beg your pardon, Captain, I didn't know you were here, I'm not properly dressed | . .

SOLIONY. It's all the same to me. Goodnight. (*Exits.*)

NATASHA. Oh, my poor dear girl, you look so tired! (*Kisses* IRINA.) You really should go to bed earlier.

IRINA. Is Bobik asleep?

NATASHA. Yes, he's sleeping. But he's a little restless. Oh, by the way, my dear, I've been meaning to have a word with you, but either you're out at work, or I've been too busy . . . I think the nursery's really too cold and damp for Bobik. But your room's just perfect for a child. Be an absolute dear and move in with Olga for a bit.

IRINA (*uncomprehending*). Move where?

The sound of a troika, with bells jingling, drawing up outside.

NATASHA. You and Olya can share for a while, and Bobik
can have your room. He's such a sweet little thing, I was
just saying to him today, 'You're my little Bobik. You're all
mine!' And he looked up at me with his darling little eyes.

The door-bell rings.

That must be Olga. She's very late.

The MAID *approaches* NATASHA *and whispers something in
her ear.*

NATASHA. Protopopov? What a strange man. Protopopov's
just arrived, and he wants to take me for a ride in his
troika. (*Laughs.*) Really, men are so funny! . . .

The door-bell rings again.

That's someone else at the door. I think I will go for a spin,
just a quarter of an hour or so . . . (*To the* MAID.) Tell him
I'll be down directly.

The door-bell rings again.

That's the bell again, it must be Olga . . . (*Exits.*)

The MAID *hurries out.* IRINA *remains seated, deep in thought.*
KULYGIN *and* OLGA *enter, followed by* VERSHININ.

KULYGIN. Well, there's a thing! And they said there was
going to be a party.

VERSHININ. That's odd — I left a short while ago, about half
an hour, and they were expecting the carnival people . . .

IRINA. They've all gone.

KULYGIN. Has Masha left too? Where did she go? And why's Protopopov waiting outside with his troika? Who's he waiting for?

IRINA. Please don't ask questions . . . I'm too tired.

KULYGIN. Oh, well, if you're in a mood . . .

OLGA. The staff meeting's only just finished, and I'm worn out. Our headmistress is off sick, and I have to take her place. I've got a splitting headache. (*Sits down.*) Andrei lost two hundred roubles at cards last night . . . The whole town's talking about it . . .

KULYGIN. Yes, I felt tired at the meeting, too.

VERSHININ. My wife took it into her head to give me a fright just now – tried to poison herself. Still, it's all over now. I can relax . . . I suppose we ought to leave. Anyway, my very best wishes. Come along, my dear chap, let's go on somewhere – I can't stay at home, I simply can't. Let's go.

KULYGIN. No, I'm too tired. Count me out. (*Rises.*) I'm exhausted. Has my wife gone home?

IRINA. I think so.

KULYGIN (*kisses* IRINA's *hand*). Well, goodnight. We've got all tomorrow and the next day off. Goodnight, everyone! (*Makes to exit.*) I'd love some tea. I was rather hoping to spend the evening in congenial company, too – *o, fallacem hominum spem!* Accusative case of exclamation . . .

VERSHININ. Well, it looks as if I'm on my own. (*Exits with* KULYGIN, *whistling.*)

OLGA. My head's aching, it really is . . . Andrei's lost
again . . . the whole town's talking . . . I'm going to lie
down. (*Makes to exit.*) I have the day off tomorrow . . .
Thank God for that! Free tomorrow and the next day . .
My head's absolutely splitting . . . (*Exits.*)

IRINA (*left alone*). They've all gone. There's no-one left.

Someone is playing a concertina outside. ANFISA *is heard singing.*

NATASHA *passes through the ballroom wearing a fur coat and
hat, followed by the* MAID.

NATASHA. I'll be back in about half an hour. I'm just going
for a little drive. (*Exits.*)

IRINA (*with intense longing*). To Moscow! Moscow! Moscow!

Curtain.

Act Three

OLGA *and* IRINA*'s room. To left and right are beds, behind screens. It is past two o'clock in the morning, and an alarm can be heard in the distance, sounding for a fire which started some time before. It is is obvious that no-one in the house has yet been to bed.* MASHA *is lying on the divan, wearing a black dress as usual.* OLGA *and* ANFISA *enter.*

ANFISA. They're sitting at the bottom of the stairs now . . . 'Why don't you go upstairs,' I says, 'You can't sit there.' And they're crying, 'We don't know where our Papa is,' they say, 'Please God he hasn't died in the fire.' That's what's on their minds! And there's more people out in the yard . . . still in their night things.

OLGA (*taking some dresses out of a cupboard*). Here, take this grey dress . . . And this one . . . And this cardigan, too . . . And here, Nanny, take this skirt . . . Oh God, this is a dreadful business – Kirsanov Street's burnt to the ground, it seems . . . And take this . . . And this . . . (*Flinging a dress into her arms.*) The Vershinins got a terrible fright, the poor things . . . Their house only just escaped. They can spend the night here, we can't let them go home . . . And poor Fedotik's lost everything, completely burned out . . .

ANFISA. Olya dear, if you would call Ferapont – I can't manage all these . . .

OLGA (*rings the bell*). I don't think they can hear . . . (*Calls through the door.*) Will someone come up here, please!

The open door reveals a window, glowing red from the fire; a fire engine is heard passing the house.

This is terrible, terrible. And so exhausting . . .

FERAPONT *enters.*

Take these downstairs, please . . . Give them to the Kolotilin girls, they're waiting in the hall . . . Give them this, too.

FERAPONT. Right, ma'am. Yes, there was a fire in Moscow too, in 1812. By God, the Frenchies didn't half get a fright!

OLGA. Now go on, quickly.

FERAPONT. Yes, ma'am. (*Exits.*)

OLGA. Nanny dear, just give everything away. We don't need it, give it all away, Nanny . . . I'm so tired, I can scarcely stand . . . We can't let the Vershinins go home . . . The girls can sleep in the drawing-room, and we can put the Colonel downstairs with the Baron . . . Fedotik can move in with the Baron, too, or go into the ballroom . . . The Doctor's drunk, it's as if he did it on purpose, he's terribly drunk, we can't put anyone in with him. And put Vershinin's wife into the drawing-room as well.

ANFISA (*exhausted*). Olya, dearest, please don't send me away! Don't send me away!

OLGA. Nanny, don't talk nonsense. Nobody's sending you anywhere.

ANFISA (*lays her head on* OLGA'*s bosom*). Oh, my dearest, darling Olya, I do my work, I work hard . . . But I'm

getting feeble,/and they'll tell me to go/'Clear off!' they'll
say./But where can I go?/Where?/I'm over eighty/– coming
up for eighty-two /. .

OLGA. Nanny,/sit down /. . You're worn out/you poor
dear /. . (*Makes* ANFISA *sit.*) Have a rest,/you've gone
quite pale/

NATASHA *enters.*

NATASHA. They're talking about setting up a fund to help
the fire victims –/a splendid idea,/don't you think?/We've
got to do what we can for the poor,/the rich have an
obligation/ Bobik and little Sophie are tucked away in bed,
fast asleep,/as if nothing's happened/ We've got people all
over the place,/the house is full of them./There's a 'flu
epidemic in the town/ I'm frightened in case the children
catch it /. .

OLGA (*not listening to her*). You can't see the fire from this
room/ it's quiet here /. .

NATASHA. Yes /. . I must look a mess/(*In front of the mirror.*)
They tell me I've put on weight /. . it's not true/
Absolutely not/ And Masha's asleep/ she's worn out/ the
poor thing /. . (*To* ANFISA, *coldly.*) How dare you sit down
in my presence!/Stand up!/Get out of here!

ANFISA *exits. A pause.*

I really can't imagine why you keep that old creature on/

OLGA (*bemused*). I'm sorry/I don't understand . . .

NATASHA. She's no use here./She's a peasant,/she ought to
be living in the country/. . . She's completely spoilt/ I must
have order in the home!/There's no room for hangers-on./

(*Strokes* OLGA'*s cheek.*) Poor thing, you're tired. Our
headmistress is tired! Yes, when my little Sophie grows up
and goes to school, I shall be afraid of you.

OLGA. I don't want to be headmistress.

NATASHA. But they're going to appoint you, Olya dear. It's
already decided.

OLGA. I'll refuse. I can't do it . . . I haven't the strength . . .
(*She takes a drink of water.*) You know, you were so rude to
Nanny just now . . . I'm sorry, but I just can't bear it . . .
I felt quite faint . . .

NATASHA (*agitatedly*) I'm sorry, Olya, I'm sorry — I didn't
mean to upset you.

MASHA *rises from the divan, picks up a pillow, and exits angrily.*

OLGA. You must understand, my dear . . . perhaps it's our
strange upbringing, but I really can't abide that. That
sort of behaviour depresses me, it makes me ill. I just feel
drained . .

NATASHA. I'm sorry, I'm sorry . . . (*Embraces her.*)

OLGA. Any form of rudeness, even the slightest thing, a
harsh word . . . it upsets me.

NATASHA. Well, I often speak out of turn, that's true, but you
must admit, my dear, she ought to be living in the country.

OLGA. But she's been with us for thirty years.

NATASHA. Yes, but she can't work any longer! Look, either I
don't understand you, or you simply don't want to
understand me. She's not fit for work, she does nothing but
sit around and sleep.

OLGA. Well, let her sit!

NATASHA (*amazed*). What do you mean, let her sit? I mean, she's a servant, for Heaven's sake. (*Tearfully.*) I just don't understand you, Olya. I have a nanny, a wet-nurse, we have a maid, a cook . . . what do we want with this old woman? What use is she?

In the distance, the fire alarm sounds.

OLGA. I think I've aged ten years tonight.

NATASHA. We'll have to come to some arrangement, Olga. You're out at school, and I'm at home — you have your schoolwork, and I have this house to run. And if I've got something to say about the servants, then I know what I'm talking about. I know whereof I speak . . . So I want that thieving old hag out of here by tomorrow! (*Stamping her foot.*) The old witch! And don't dare cross me! Just don't dare! (*Recovering her composure.*) The truth is, Olga, unless you move downstairs, we're going to be quarrelling all the time. It's terrible.

KULYGIN *enters.*

KULYGIN. Where's Masha? It's time we went home. The fire seems to be dying down. (*Stretches.*) There's only one part of town burnt, although with that wind, it looked at first as if the whole lot would go up. (*Sits down.*) Oh, I'm so tired. Dearest Olga . . . You know, I often think, if it hadn't been for Masha, I should've married you. You're so kind. Yes, I'm exhausted. (*Listens.*)

OLGA. What is it?

KULYGIN. The Doctor's been hitting the bottle, he's drunk

as a lord. You'd think he'd done it on purpose! (*Stands up.*) This is him now, I think. Isn't it? Yes, here he comes . . . (*Laughs.*) The old rogue . . . I'm going to hide from him . . . (*Goes over to the cupboard and stands in the corner.*) He's such a rascal.

OLGA. He hasn't touched a drop in two years, and now he suddenly has to get drunk . . . (*She goes with* NATASHA *to the far end of the room.*)

CHEBUTYKIN *enters, and crosses the room without staggering, as if he were sober. He stops, looks round, then goes to the washbasin and washes his hands.*)

CHEBUTYKIN (*gloomily*). To hell with the lot of them . . . damn them . . . They think because I'm a doctor I can cure all their ailments, but I know absolutely nothing, I've forgotten all I ever knew, I don't remember a thing, not a damn thing.

OLGA *and* NATASHA *make their exit, unnoticed by* CHEBUTYKIN.

To hell with them! Last Wednesday I was attending a woman in Zasyp Street – she died, and it was my fault she died. Yes . . . Maybe I knew a few things twenty-five years ago, but now I can't remember a thing. Not a thing. Maybe I'm not even human, I'm just pretending I've got arms, and legs . . . and a head. Maybe I don't exist, yes, maybe I only imagine I walk, eat, and sleep . . . (*Starts crying.*) Oh, if only I didn't exist! (*Stops crying, then morosely.*) Dear God . . . There was some talk at the club a couple of days ago . . . Shakespeare, Voltaire, and so on . . . I've never read them, not a word, but I tried to look as if I had.

And the others were doing the same. It's contemptible. Degrading. And I got to thinking about that woman I'd killed on Wednesday . . . and it all came back to me, and I felt so vile, so downright rotten . . . I had to go and get a drink . . .

IRINA, VERSHININ *and* TUZENBAKH *enter.* TUZENBAKH *is wearing a fashionable new civilian suit.*

IRINA. We can sit down here. Nobody'll come in.

VERSHININ. Well, if it hadn't been for the military, the whole town would've gone up in flames. They did splendidly! (*Rubs his hands in satisfaction.*) They're a fine bunch, salt of the earth!

KULYGIN (*Goes up to them.*) What time is it, anyone?

TUZENBAKH. It's after three already. It's getting light.

IRINA. They're all sitting in the ballroom, no-one wants to leave. And that Soliony of yours is there, too. (*To* CHEBUTYKIN.) You ought to go back to bed, Doctor.

CHEBUTYKIN. I'm fine, ma'am . . . Thank you, ma'am . . . (*Stroking his beard.*)

KULYGIN (*laughs*). You've had one too many, Ivan Romanych! (*Slaps him on the back.*) Bravo! *In vino veritas*, as the Romans used to say.

TUZENBAKH. People keep asking me to organise a concert, in aid of the fire victims.

IRINA. Yes, but who'll play . . .

TUZENBAKH. We could do it, if we really wanted. There's Masha, for instance. She plays the piano beautifully . . .

KULYGIN. She does indeed!

IRINA. She's forgotten how. She hasn't played in three years . . . maybe four.

TUZENBAKH. There's absolutely nobody in this town who appreciates music, not a soul. However, I do, and I tell you this – Masha is a superb pianist, practically a genius.

KULYGIN. You're quite right, Baron. And I love Masha so much. She's a wonderful woman.

TUZENBAKH. To be able to play so gloriously, and to know at the same time that nobody, absolutely nobody appreciates it!

KULYGIN (sighs). Yes, indeed . . . But would it be proper for Masha to take part in a concert?

A pause.

I mean, I know nothing about such matters. It may be perfectly fine. Our headmaster is a good man, I must say, a thoroughly decent man, extremely clever, but he does have certain views . . . Of course, it's not his concern, but I'll mention it to him all the same, if you don't mind . . .

CHEBUTYKIN *has picked up a china clock and is inspecting it.*

VERSHININ. I got absolutely filthy at the fire, you wouldn't believe it.

A pause.

Incidentally, I heard yesterday they're thinking of transferring our brigade to some outpost or other. Poland, they're saying, or possibly Siberia.

TUZENBAKH. Yes, that's what I heard. Well, well – this town'll be deserted then.

IRINA. And we're leaving too!

CHEBUTYKIN (*drops the clock, which smashes on the floor*). Smithereens!

A pause. Everyone is upset and embarrassed.

KULYGIN (*Starts picking up the pieces*). Oh, Ivan Romanych, Ivan Romanych – breaking such a valuable object, really! I shall give you a C-minus for conduct.

IRINA. That was our mother's clock.

CHEBUTYKIN. Maybe . . . Well, what if it was? Maybe I didn't break it, maybe it just looks as if I did. Maybe we don't even exist, and only imagine we do. I don't know anything, nobody knows a damn thing. (*At the door.*) What are you staring at? Natasha's having an affair with Proto-popov, and you can't see it . . . You're all sitting here, seeing nothing, and Natasha's having an affair with Pro-topopov . . . (*Sings.*) 'Oh, lady, please accept this fruit . . .' (*Exits.*)

VERSHININ. Yes . . . (*Laughs.*) It's a strange world we live in.

A pause.

You know, when the fire broke out, I rushed home, and when I got there I could see our house was still intact, and out of danger, but my two little girls were standing at the door, in nothing but their nightgowns, their mother wasn't with them, there were people dashing around everywhere, horses and dogs, and I can't describe the alarm and terror, the pathetic look on those little faces. My heart almost stopped at the sight of them. Dear God, I thought, what have those little girls still to suffer in the course of a long life? I snatched them up and started running, and all the time I kept thinking – what more will they have to suffer in this world?

The fire alarm sounds. A pause.

Then I arrive here, and their mother's shouting and screaming.

MASHA *enters, carrying her pillow, and sits on the divan.*

Yes, when my little girls were standing at the door in their nightgowns, and the whole street was glowing red with fire, there was a hellish uproar, and it came into my mind that things like this used to happen many years ago, when some enemy would suddenly invade us, looting and burning . . . But when you come right down to it, there's a world of difference between then and now. And given a little more time, say, two or three hundred years, people will look back on us with the same horror and scorn, our present-day life will seem hard and awkward, it'll seem very uncomfortable and bizarre. Oh yes, what a life that's going to be! (*Laughs.*) I'm sorry, I'm getting carried away again. But don't stop me, please – I desperately want to talk, it's the kind of mood I'm in . . .

A pause.

It looks as if everyone's asleep. Anyway, as I was saying: life will be wonderful! We can only imagine what it'll be like . . . I mean, there are only the three of you in this town now, but in future generations there'll be more, many, many more, and the time's coming when everything will change, people will live as you'd like them to, you'll grow old eventually, and there'll be other people born, even better than you . . . (*Laughs.*) Oh yes, I'm in a really good mood today. I have the most damnable desire to live! . . . (*Sings.*) 'To Love all ages humbly bow, her promptings do each heart endow . . .' (*Laughs.*)

MASHA. Tram-tam-tam . . .

VERSHININ. Tam-tam . . .

MASHA. Tra-ra-ra?

VERSHININ. Tra-ta-ta. (*Laughs.*)

  FEDOTIK *enters.*

FEDOTIK (*dancing*). It's all gone! All gone! Burnt to the ground!

  Laughter.

IRINA. What's funny about that? Is everything burnt?

FEDOTIK (*laughs*). Yes, gone up in smoke, everything. Not a thing left. My guitar, my camera, all my letters, all gone . . . I was going to give you a little notebook, that's burnt too.

  SOLIONY *enters.*

IRINA. No, please, Captain Soliony, please go away. You can't come in here.

SOLIONY. So why can the Baron come in, and I can't?

VERSHININ. Actually, we ought to be leaving. How's the fire?

SOLIONY. It's dying down, they say. No, it's positively

peculiar – the Baron's allowed in here, and I'm not. (*Takes out a bottle of scent and sprinkles himself with it.*)

VERSHININ. Tram-tam-tam?

MASHA. Tram-tam.

VERSHININ (*laughs, then to* SOLIONY). Let's go into the ballroom.

SOLIONY. All right. But we shan't forget this. (*Looking pointedly at* TUZENBAKH.) 'This moral I might make more clear, but that would vex the geese, I fear . . . ' Cheep! Cheep! Cheep! (*Exits with* VERSHININ *and* FEDOTIK.)

IRINA. That Soliony's smoked the place out . . . (*Bewildered.*) The Baron's asleep. Baron, wake up!

TUZENBAKH (*coming to.*) Oh, I'm so tired still . . . Yes, the brick-works . . . No, I'm not talking in my sleep, I'll be starting work soon, in a brick-works, it's all arranged. (*To* IRINA, *tenderly.*) You're so pale and lovely, quite enchanting . . . It's as if your face lights up the night air, like a moonbeam . . . You're so sad, dissatisfied with life . . . Oh, come with me, Irina, we'll go away and work together! . . .

MASHA. Baron, please leave.

TUZENBAKH (*laughing*). You're here? I didn't see you. (*Kisses* IRINA's *hand*) . . . Goodbye, I'm going . . . You know, I look at you now, and it all comes back to me, a long time ago on your name-day, how bright and cheerful you were then, talking about the joys of work . . . And what a happy life I could see ahead of me . . . But where is it? (*He kisses her hand.*) There are tears in your eyes. You should go to bed, it's getting light already . . . almost morning . . . Oh, if only I could give my life for you, Irina!

MASHA. Baron, please go. For heaven's sake . . .

TUZENBAKH. I'm going, I'm going . . . (*Exits.*)

MASHA (*lies down*). Fyodor? Are you asleep?

KULYGIN. Pardon?

MASHA. You ought to go home.

KULYGIN. Darling Masha, my dear, sweet Masha . . .

IRINA. She's exhausted. Let her rest, Fedya.

KULYGIN. I'm just going . . . My wife's so good and kind . . . I love you, my one and only . . .

MASHA (*irritated*). *Amo, amas, amat, amamus, amatis, amant* . . .

KULYGIN (*laughs*). Really, an amazing woman! Yes, we got married seven years ago, and it seems like only yesterday. That's the truth. I say again, you're an amazing woman, Masha. And I'm so very, very happy!

MASHA. And I'm so very, very bored! . . . (*Sits up.*) You know, I can't get it out of my head . . . It's simply disgraceful. It's preying on my mind, I can't keep silent. I'm talking about Andrei . . . He's mortgaged this house to the bank, and his wife's pocketed the money. I mean, the house isn't just his, it belongs to all four of us! He surely knows that, if he's got any decency.

KULYGIN. Masha, why bring this up now? What does it matter? Andrei owes everybody money, Heaven help him.

MASHA. It's a disgrace, even so. (*Lies down again.*)

KULYGIN. Masha, it's not as if we're poor. I have my work, I teach at the school, and give private lessons . . . I'm an honest, simple man . . . *Omnia mea mecum porto*, as they say.

MASHA. I don't need anything, it's just so unfair, it makes me angry.

A pause.

Fyodor, go home, please.

KULYGIN (*embraces her*). You're tired! Have a little rest for a half-hour or so, and I'll wait downstairs. Try and sleep . . . (*Exits.*) I'm so very, very happy . . .

IRINA. It's true enough, our Andrei's become so mean-minded – the spirit's gone right out of him, he's grown so *old* with that woman. He had his sights set on a professorship at one time, and there he was yesterday, bragging because at long last they'd made him a member of the district council! He's a member of the council, and the chairman's Protopopov . . . The whole town's talking about it, laughing behind his back – he's the only one who doesn't know . . . Yes, and when everybody rushes out to help with the fire, he sits in his room, not the least bit concerned. Playing his fiddle. (*Agitated.*) It's terrible, terrible! (*Begins to cry.*) I can't stand it, I can't take any more of this! . . . I can't, I can't . . .

OLGA *enters, to tidy up her dressing-table.* IRINA *is sobbing loudly.*

Oh, throw me out, put me out of here, I can't stand it any more!

OLGA (*alarmed*). What's the matter, what is it? Irina, dearest!

IRINA (*sobbing*). Where has it all gone? Where? Where is it?
Oh God in Heaven! I've forgotten everything, everything . . It's all gone right out of my head . . . I can't
remember the Italian for 'window', or 'ceiling' . . . I'm
forgetting more and more each day, life's passing me by,
and it'll never return, we'll never get to Moscow, we'll
never leave here, I know we won't . . .

OLGA. Oh, my poor darling . . .

IRINA (*trying to control herself*). Oh, I'm just so miserable . . .
I can't work, I won't work, I've had enough of it! First
I worked in the telegraph office, now I have a job with
the town council, and I despise everything they give me to
do . . . I'm twenty-four already, I've been working for ages,
my brain's dried up, I've become thin, and old, and ugly –
there's no satisfaction in any of it, absolutely none, and
time's passing, and I feel as if I'm moving further and
further away from a genuine, beautiful life, and heading
into some kind of abyss. I'm in despair, I don't know why
I'm still alive, why I haven't killed myself before now, I
don't understand it . . .

OLGA. Don't cry, darling, don't cry . . . It hurts me . . .

IRINA. I won't, I won't cry . . . Enough . . . Look, I've
stopped crying . . . It's over . . .

OLGA. Oh, my dear, I'm speaking to you now as a sister, as a
friend . . . If you want my advice, you should marry the
Baron.

IRINA *quietly weeps.*

After all, you respect him, you think highly of him . . .
True, he's not good-looking, but he's a decent man,

clean-living/. . . I mean, women don't marry for love, they do it out of duty/At least,/that's what I think/and I'd marry without love./I'd marry anyone that asked me/as long as he was a decent person/ I'd even marry an old man/. . .

IRINA. I kept waiting,/waiting for us to move to Moscow, and I'd meet my true love there./I've dreamt about him,/loved him/. . . But it's turned out to be nonsense,/all of it . . .

OLGA (*hugs her sister*). Oh, my dear, darling sister/I understand everything./When the Baron left the service, and came to see us in his civilian clothes, he looked so awful that I actually started to cry/. . . And he asked me/ 'Why are you crying?'/What could I tell him?/But if it's God's will that he should marry you, I'd be very happy.) That'd be quite different.

NATASHA *crosses the stage from right to left in silence, holding a candle.*

MASHA (*sits up*). The way she's going around, you'd think it was her that started the fire.

OLGA. And you're silly, Masha. You're the silliest person in this family/ If you'll forgive my saying.

A pause.

MASHA. I've a confession to make, my dear sisters./ Something on my conscience/ I'm going to confess to you, and to no-one else, ever ./. . . I'll tell you now./(*Quietly.*) It's my secret,/but you ought to know ./. . . I can't keep it any longer . . .

A pause.

I'm in love . . . I'm in love with that man . . . You saw him just now . . . Oh, why not come out with it? I'm in love with Vershinin . . .

OLGA (*goes behind her screen*). That's enough, I'm not listening to you anyway!

MASHA. I can't help it! (*Clutching her head.*) At first I thought he was strange, then I felt sorry for him . . . eventually I fell in love with him . . . I fell in love with his voice, the things he said, his unhappy life, his two little girls . . .

OLGA (*from behind the screen*). I don't care, I can't hear you. You can say whatever stupid things you like, I'm not listening.

MASHA. Oh, Olga, it's you that's stupid. I'm in love, it's fate. It's my destiny . . . And he loves me . . . It's frightening, isn't it? Is it wrong? (*Takes* IRINA *by the hand, draws her close.*) Oh, my dear Irina, how are we going to survive? What's to become of us? . . . You know, when you read a love story you think, well, this is all old-hat, everybody knows this. But when you fall in love yourself, it's obvious that nobody knows anything, we each have to work it out on our own. Oh, my dearest sisters . . . I've confessed to you, now I'll keep silent . . . I'll be like Gogol's madman . . . The rest is silence . . .

ANDREI *enters, followed by* FERAPONT.

ANDREI (*testily*). What is it you want? I can't understand you.

FERAPONT (*at the door, impatiently*). Master Andrei, I've told you half a dozen times.

ANDREI. In the first place, I'm not Master Andrei to you, but Your Honour!

FERAPONT. Your Honour, the firemen want permission to drive through the orchard to the river. Otherwise they've got to go all the way round, and that's a terrible job.

ANDREI. All right. Tell them it's all right.

FERAPONT *exits.*

Honestly, they get on my nerves. Where's Olga?

OLGA *emerges from behind the screen.*

I came to ask you for the cupboard key, I seem to have lost mine. That little key you have.

OLGA *silently hands him the key.* IRINA *goes behind her own screen. A pause.*

What a huge fire! It's dying down now. Damn it, that Ferapont really annoyed me, I came out with something stupid . . . Your Honour, indeed!

A pause.

Why don't you say something, Olya?

A pause.

Look, it's time we put a stop to all this nonsense, all this sulking for no reason. You're here, Masha's here, Irina, well, that's just fine – we can get to the bottom of it now, once and for all. Exactly what is it you have against me? Come on, tell me.

OLGA. Leave it, Andryusha. We'll talk about it tomorrow. (*Upset.*) What a dreadful night it's been!

ANDREI (*He is rather embarrassed*). Don't get upset. I'm asking you perfectly calmly: what have you got against me? Come right out with it.

VERSHININ *is heard off-stage: 'Tram-tam-tam!'*

MASHA (*stands up, then loudly*). Tra-ta-ta! (*To* OLGA.) Goodbye, Olga, and God bless you. (*Goes behind the screen, kisses* IRINA.) Sleep well . . . Goodbye, Andrei. Just leave them, they're exhausted . . . you can have it out with them tomorrow. (*Exits.*)

OLGA. Yes, Andrei, let's put it off till tomorrow . . . (*She goes behind her screen.*) It's time we were in bed.

ANDREI. I'll say my piece and then I'll go. Directly . . . In the first place, you've got something against my wife Natasha, and I've been aware of that since the day of our wedding. Natasha's a fine, honest woman, upright and honourable – that's my opinion. I love and respect my wife, do you understand? I respect her, and I insist that other people respect her too. I'll say it again, she's a decent, honest woman, and all your complaints about her, I'm sorry to say, are nothing but sheer bloody-mindedness.

A pause.

And secondly, it's as if you're annoyed at me for not being a professor, for not being an academic. But I serve on the district council, I'm a member of the executive, and in my view that's just as exalted and sacred an office as any academic post. I'm a member of the district council, yes, and proud of it, if you must know . . .

A pause.

Thirdly . . . I've something more to say . . . I mortgaged the house without asking your permission . . . Well, that was wrong of me, and I'm asking you to forgive me . . . I was driven to it by debt . . . thirty-five thousand . . . I've stopped gambling, gave it up ages ago. The only thing I can say in my own defence is that you girls have an annuity, and I've never had anything . . . no income, I mean . . .

A pause.

KULYGIN (*at the door*). Isn't Masha here? (*Anxiously.*) Where can she be? That's odd . . . (*Exits.*)

ANDREI. They're not listening. Natasha's a first-class, honest person. (*Paces up and down in silence a few moments, then stops.*) When I got married, I thought we'd be so happy . . . all of us . . . But oh, my God . . . (*Begins to cry.*) Oh, my dear sisters, my good, kind sisters, don't listen to me, don't believe a word of it . . . (*Exits.*)

KULYGIN (*appearing anxiously at the door*). Where's Masha? She's still not here? Most peculiar . . . (*Exits.*)

The fire alarm is heard. The stage seems deserted.

IRINA (*from behind her screen*). Olya! Who's that knocking on the floor?

OLGA. It's the Doctor. He's drunk.

IRINA. What a dreadful night!

A pause. She looks out from behind her screen.

Olya! Have you heard? The brigade's to be transferred, somewhere far away.

OLGA. It's just a rumour.

IRINA. We'll be left on our own, then . . . oh, Olya!

OLGA. What is it now?

IRINA. Listen, my dearest – I respect the Baron, I think highly of him, he's a fine man, and I shall marry him, yes, just as long as we go to Moscow! Oh, please, please, let's go to Moscow! There's nowhere in the world like Moscow! We've got to go, Olya, we must!

Curtain.

Act Four

The old garden of the PROZOROV *house. A long avenue of fir-trees, leading to a river, with a wooded opposite bank. To the right is the verandah of the house, and a table with bottles and glasses – they have obviously been drinking champagne. It is mid-day. Now and again people stroll through the garden on their way from the street to the river. Five or six soldiers march quickly past.* CHEBUTYKIN *is sitting in an armchair, in a benign frame of mind, a mood which does not leave him throughout the entire act. He is waiting to be summoned somewhere, wearing his army cap, and carrying a walking-stick.* IRINA *and* KULYGIN, *the latter with a medal hung round his neck, and his moustaches now shaved off, are standing on the terrace with* TUZENBAKH, *bidding farewell to* FEDOTIK *and* RODE, *who are coming down the steps, dressed in their parade uniforms.*

TUZENBAKH (*embraces* FEDOTIK). You're a good chap, Fedotik, we've got on well together. (*Embraces* RODE.) And you too, Rodé . . . Goodbye, my dear friend!

IRINA. *Au revoir!*

FEDOTIK. No, not *au revoir*, it's goodbye, I'm afraid – we'll never see each other again.

KULYGIN. Who knows? (*Wipes his eyes, smiling.*) Look at this, I'm crying too!

IRINA. We'll meet again some day.

FEDOTIK. What, in ten or fifteen years, say? We'll barely

recognise each other by then, we'll shake hands very coldly . . . (*Takes a photograph.*) Now, hold still . . . One last time.

RODE (*embraces* TUZENBAKH). We shan't ever meet again . . . (*Kisses* IRINA's *hand.*) Thank you for all you've done for us. Thank you.

FEDOTIK (*irritated*). Oh, do stand still!

TUZENBAKH. If it's God's will, we'll meet again. But you will write to us, though. Be sure and write.

RODE (*looking round at the garden*). Farewell, trees! (*Shouts.*) Coo-eee! Coo-eee!

A pause.

Farewell, echo!

KULYGIN. With any luck, you'll get married there in Poland . . . And your Polish wife'll fling her arms round you and say, 'Kohane! My darleeng!' (*Laughs.*)

FEDOTIK (*glances at his watch*). We've less than an hour left. Soliony's the only one in our unit going by barge, the rest of us are with the infantry. There's three battery divisions moving out today, another three tomorrow – peace and quiet'll descend upon the town.

TUZENBAKH. And deadly boredom.

RODE. So where's Mariya Sergeyevna?

KULYGIN. Masha's in the garden.

FEDOTIK. We must say goodbye to her.

RODE. Goodbye. I'd better go, before I start crying . . .

(*Quickly embraces* TUZENBAKH *and* KULYGIN, *and kisses* IRINA's *hand.*) We've had such good times here . . .

FEDOTIK (*to* KULYGIN). This is for you, a keepsake . . . a notebook and pencil. We'll walk down this way to the river . . .

They move off, turning to look back now and again.

RODE (*shouts*). Coo-eee! Coo-eee!

KULYGIN (*shouts*). Goodbye!

FEDOTIK *and* RODE *encounter* MASHA *in the background, and make their goodbyes to her. She exits along with them.*

IRINA. They've gone. (*She sits down on the bottom step of the verandah.*)

CHEBUTYKIN. They forgot to say goodbye to me.

IRINA. And what about you?

CHEBUTYKIN. I forgot as well. Anyway, I'll be seeing them again soon, I'm leaving tomorrow. Yes . . . Just one more day. And in a year from now when they retire me, I'll come back here and live out my life near you . . . Just one short year to go until my pension . . . (*He puts one newspaper in his pocket, takes out another.*) I'll come back here to you, and turn over a new leaf . . . I'll be so quiet, and well . . . well-behaved, and respectable . . .

IRINA. You really ought to turn over a new leaf, my dear. You really should try.

CHEBUTYKIN. Yes. I know. (*Sings quietly.*) Ta-ra-ra boom-dee-ay, ta-ra-ra boom-dee-ay . . .

KULYGIN. You're incorrigible, Doctor. Quite incorrigible!

CHEBUTYKIN. Yes, I should've come to you for lessons. You'd have straightened me out.

IRINA. Fyodor's shaved off his moustaches. I can't look at him!

KULYGIN. What's the matter?

CHEBUTYKIN. I wish I could say what your phizzog looks like now, but I can't.

KULYGIN. Oh, come on, it's the done thing nowadays, the *modus vivendi*. Our headmaster's shaved off his whiskers, and since I've been made deputy, I've shaved mine off too. Nobody likes it, but I don't care. I'm happy. With or without whiskers, I'm a happy man. (*Sits down.*)

At the bottom of the garden ANDREI *is pushing a pram with a sleeping baby in it.*

IRINA. Doctor, dear Ivan Romanych, I'm terribly worried. You were in town yesterday, on the boulevard – tell me what happened there?

CHEBUTYKIN. What happened? Nothing. Nothing important. (*Reads his newspaper.*) What's it matter anyway?

KULYGIN. According to the story, Soliony and the Baron bumped into each other on the boulevard outside the theatre . . .

TUZENBAKH. Oh, stop, that's enough. Honestly! (*Waves his hand dismissively and goes into the house.*)

KULYGIN. Yes, outside the theatre . . . Soliony started picking on the Baron, and he lost his temper and insulted Soliony . . .

CHEBUTYKIN. I don't know – it's all bunkum.

KULYGIN. I heard about a teacher in a seminary once, who
wrote 'bunkum' on a student's essay, and he thought it was
a Latin word! (*Laughs.*) That's really funny. Yes, it seems
Soliony's in love with Irina, and he's conceived the most
terrible spite against the Baron . . . Well, that's
understandable. Irina's a very pretty girl. And she's so like
Masha, always deep in thought. You've a gentler nature,
though, Irina. Of course, Masha has a very nice nature
too. Yes, I do love Masha.

*From the far end of the garden, off-stage, someone is calling: 'Coo-
eee! Coo-eee!'*

IRINA (*gives a start*). Everything seems to frighten me today.

A pause.

Well, I've got everything packed, and I'll send off my luggage
after lunch. The Baron and I are getting married
tomorrow, and we'll leave for the brick-works tomorrow
afternoon. I'll be teaching at the school the very next day,
beginning a new life, with God's help! You know, when I
passed the exam to be a teacher, I actually cried for joy, I
was so happy . . .

A pause.

The cart'll be here soon for my things.

KULYGIN. Well, that's as maybe, but it somehow doesn't
seem serious. A lot of ideas, yes, but not much serious
thought. Still, I wish you well, from the bottom of my
heart.

CHEBUTYKIN (*deeply moved*). My dear, darling girl . . . My

sweet child . . . You're going so far away, we'll never catch you up . . . And I'm left behind, like some migrating bird that's grown too old to fly. But fly away, my darlings, fly away, and God be with you!

A pause.

You know, Kulygin, you shouldn't have shaved off your moustache.

KULYGIN. Oh, that's enough from you. (*Sighs.*) Yes, the soldiers are leaving today, and soon everything'll be back to normal. You know, people can say what they like, Masha's a fine, honest woman. I love her very much, and I'm thankful the way things have turned out. People have such different fates . . . There's a man called Kozyrev who works in the excise office. He was at school with me, but they expelled him from the fifth form because he couldn't make head or tail of *ut consecutivum*. He's desperately poor now, and sick, and whenever I meet him, I say, 'Hello, *ut consecutivum*!' 'Yes,' he says, '*Consecutivum*, that's it exactly!' and then he starts coughing . . . Whereas I've been lucky all my life, I'm a happy man, I've even been awarded the Order of St. Stanislaus, Second Class, and now I'm teaching others that same *ut consecutivum*. Of course, I'm a clever man, cleverer than most, but that's no guarantee of happiness . . .

Inside the house, someone is playing 'The Maiden's Prayer'.

IRINA. And tomorrow evening I'll no longer have to listen to that 'Maiden's Prayer', or run into Protopopov . . .

A pause.

You know Protopopov's sitting in the drawing-room; he's here again today.

KULYGIN. Hasn't our headmistress arrived yet?

IRINA. No. They've gone to fetch her. Oh, if you only knew how hard it's been, living here alone, without Olya . . . She stays at the school now, she's headmistress, she's busy the whole day, but I'm on my own, bored stiff, with nothing to do, and that hateful room I have to live in . . . Anyway, I've made up my mind: if it's not God's will I should go to Moscow, then so be it. It's fate. There's nothing I can do about it . . . It's in God's hands, and that's the truth. The Baron's proposed to me . . . Well, why not? I've thought it over and decided to accept him. He's a fine man, an extraordinarily fine man . . . And it's as if my heart's suddenly sprouted wings, I feel bright and cheerful, and I'm longing to get to work again . . . Only something happened yesterday, there's some sort of mystery, and it's preying on my mind . . .

CHEBUTYKIN. Bunkum.

NATASHA (*through the window*). It's our headmistress!

KULYGIN. Our headmistress has arrived. Let's go inside.

Goes into the house with IRINA.

CHEBUTYKIN (*reading his newspaper, quietly singing*). Ta-ra-ra boom-dee-ay . . . ta-ra-ra boom-dee-ay . . .

MASHA *goes up to him.* ANDREI *is still wheeling the pram in the background.*

MASHA. Sitting all by himself, not a care in the world.

CHEBUTYKIN. What of it?

MASHA. Nothing . . . (*Sits down.*)

   A pause.

   Were you in love with my mother?

CHEBUTYKIN. Very much.

MASHA. And did she love you?

CHEBUTYKIN (*after a pause*). I don't remember.

MASHA. Is my man here? That's what our cook, Martha, used to call her policeman – my man. Is my man here?

CHEBUTYKIN. Not yet.

MASHA. You know, when you have to snatch your happiness in little bits, and then you lose it, as I'm doing, you become gradually coarser, you become a shrew. . . (*Points to her bosom.*) I'm seething inside, in here . . . (*Looking at her brother ANDREI, pushing the pram.*) Look at our dear brother, Andrei . . . All our hopes lie in ruins. Like a great bell. It took thousands of people to raise it, at the expense of vast amounts of money and labour, then it suddenly fell down and shattered. Just like that, without rhyme or reason. That was Andrei . . .

ANDREI. Just when are we going to have some peace in this house? It's so noisy.

CHEBUTYKIN. Soon enough. (*Looks at his watch.*) This is an old-fashioned watch, it chimes the hour . . . (*He winds it up, and it chimes.*) The first, second and fifth battalions are leaving at one o'clock sharp . . .

A pause.

And I go tomorrow.

ANDREI. For good?

CHEBUTYKIN. I don't know. I might come back next year. Although, God knows, it hardly matters . . .

In the distance, someone is playing a harp and violin.

ANDREI. The town'll be deserted. Snuffed out like a candle.

A pause.

Something happened outside the theatre last night. They're all talking about it.

CHEBUTYKIN. It was nothing. Foolishness. Soliony started picking on the Baron, the Baron flared up and insulted him. In the end, Soliony had to challenge him to a duel. (*Looks at his watch.*) It's just about time now . . . Half-past twelve in the Crown forest. You can see it from here, the other side of the river . . . Bang-bang! (*Laughs.*) Soliony fancies himself as Lermontov, even writes poetry . . . Joking aside, this'll be his third duel.

MASHA. Whose?

CHEBUTYKIN. Soliony's.

MASHA. And what about the Baron?

CHEBUTYKIN. What about the Baron?

A pause.

MASHA. I don't know, my head's in a whirl . . . But I don't think it should be allowed. He might wound the Baron, or even kill him.

CHEBUTYKIN. The Baron's a fine chap, but what's one Baron more or less – it hardly matters, does it? Let them fight! Who cares?

Beyond the garden, someone shouts: 'Coo-eee! Coo-eee!'

Oh, let him wait. That's Skvortsov shouting, one of the seconds. He's down there in the boat.

A pause.

ANDREI. Well, I think fighting a duel, or being present at one, even as a doctor, is downright immoral.

CHEBUTYKIN. No, it just seems that way. We're not here, there's nothing here, we don't exist. We only seem to exist. And what difference does it make anyway?

MASHA. That's how they go on the whole day, talk, talk, talk . . . (*Makes to exit.*) You live in a climate where it snows at the drop of a hat, and on top of it all, these stupid conversations . . . (*Stops.*) I'm not going into the house, I can't go in there. Tell me when Vershinin arrives . . . (*Walks off down the avenue.*) The birds are already migrating . . . (*Looks up at the sky.*) Swans, or geese . . . Lucky creatures . . . (*Exits.*)

ANDREI. This house'll be empty soon. The officers are leaving, you're leaving, my sister's getting married . . . I'll be left on my own.

CHEBUTYKIN. What about your wife?

FERAPONT *enters with some papers.*

ANDREI. My wife's my wife. Oh, she's an honest, decent woman, good-natured, I suppose, but there's something about her that reduces her to the level of some small, blind, furry animal. At any rate, she's not human. I'm telling you this as a friend, the only person I can open my heart to. I love Natasha, I do, but at times she seems so incredibly vulgar, and then I'm confused. I just can't understand why I love her, or at any rate *did* love her . . .

CHEBUTYKIN (*stands up*). Listen, my friend, I'm leaving tomorrow. We may never see each other again, so here's my advice to you. Put on your hat, take up your stick, and walk away . . . walk away, and keep walking, without so much as a backward glance. The further the better.

In the background, SOLIONY *goes past with two officers. He catches sight of* CHEBUTYKIN *and turns towards him. The officers continue on.*

SOLIONY. Time we were going, Doctor. It's already half-past. (*Greets* ANDREI.)

CHEBUTYKIN. I'm coming, I'm coming. I'm fed up with all of you. (*To* ANDREI.) Andrei, dear chap, if anyone's looking for me, tell them I'll be back presently . . . (*Sighs.*) Oh, dear . . .

SOLIONY. 'Before he had time to gasp, the bear had him in its grasp!' (*Walks along with* CHEBUTYKIN.) What are you moaning about, old man?

CHEBUTYKIN. What d'you mean?

SOLIONY. How's your health?

CHEBUTYKIN (*testily*). I'm fit as a fiddle.

SOLIONY. Don't upset yourself, old man. I shall indulge myself a little. I'll just wing him, like a woodcock. (*Takes out his scent-bottle and sprinkles some on his hands.*) I've used up a whole bottle of this today, and my hands still stink. They smell like a corpse.

A pause.

Anyway . . . Do you remember the lines? 'But he, rebellious, seeks the storm, as if in storms lay peace . . . '

CHEBUTYKIN. Yes. 'Before he had time to gasp, the bear had him in its grasp . . . ' (*Exits with* SOLIONY.)

Shouts are heard again: 'Coo-eee! Coo-eee!' ANDREI *and* FERAPONT *enter.*

FERAPONT. There's papers to be signed, sir . . .

ANDREI. Leave me alone! Go away, for Heaven's sake! (*Exits with the pram.*)

FERAPONT. I mean, that's what papers are for, for signing . . . (*Walks off into the background.*)

IRINA *enters with* TUZENBAKH, *wearing a straw hat.* KULYGIN *crosses the stage, calling, 'Coo-eee, Masha! Coo-eee!'*

TUZENBAKH. I think he's the only person in town who's glad the army's leaving.

IRINA. That's understandable.

A pause.

The town'll be empty now.

TUZENBAKH (*glancing at his watch*). Listen, darling, I'll be back in a minute . . .

IRINA. Where are you going?

TUZENBAKH. I've got to go into town . . . to see off my comrades.

IRINA. That's not true . . . Nikolai, why are you so distracted today?

A pause.

What happened outside the theatre?

TUZENBAKH (*with a gesture of impatience*) I'll be back within the hour, by your side, Irina. (*Kisses her hand.*) My dearest darling . . . (*Gazing into her eyes.*) You know, five years have gone by, since I fell in love with you, and I still can't get used to it. You grow more beautiful every day. That wonderful, fascinating hair. Those beautiful eyes. And tomorrow I'll take you away, and we'll work, we'll be rich, all my dreams will come true. And you'll be happy, Irina. There's only one thing, just one: you don't love me.

IRINA. There's nothing I can do about that. I'll be your wife, I'll be faithful and obedient, but I don't love you. I can't help it. (*Weeps.*) I've never loved anyone. Oh, I used to dream about love, I dreamt about love all the time, day and night, but it's as if my heart were a valuable grand piano, which someone's locked up, and they've lost the key. (*A pause.*) You look worried.

TUZENBAKH. I didn't sleep last night. Not that there's anything to fear in my life, nothing I'm worried about, but that lost key tears me apart, it won't let me sleep . . . Speak to me, Irina.

A pause.

Say something . . .

IRINA. What? What can I say? Everything around us is so mysterious, the old trees stand silently . . . (*She lays her head on his breast.*)

TUZENBAKH. Speak to me, say anything . . .

IRINA. What can I say?

TUZENBAKH. Anything.

IRINA. Don't, please!

A pause.

TUZENBAKH. You know, it's strange how the silliest things in life can suddenly seem so important, for no particular reason. You laugh at them the same as always, you can see them for the trivial things they are, but you carry on regardless, as if you hadn't the power to stop. Well, let's not talk about that. I feel quite elated. It's as if I'm seeing these fir-trees, and maples and birches, for the very first time, as if everything's watching me, and just waiting. How beautiful the trees are, and how beautiful the life around them should be!

A shout is heard: 'Coo-eee! Coo-eee!'

It's time I was going . . . Look, that tree's dead, but it's still swaying in the wind with the others. In the same way, I think if I die, I'll still be a part of life, come what may. Goodbye, my darling . . . (*Kisses her hand.*) Oh, those papers you gave me are lying on my desk, under the calendar.

IRINA. I'm coming with you.

TUZENBAKH (*hastily*). No, no. (*Walks off quickly, and stops in the avenue.*) Irina . . .

IRINA. Yes?

TUZENBAKH (*unsure what to say*). I haven't had coffee yet. Ask them to make me some, will you? (*Hurriedly exits.*)

> IRINA *stands deep in thought, then goes upstage to sit on a swing.* ANDREI *enters, pushing the pram.* FERAPONT *then appears.*

FERAPONT. I mean, they're not my papers, sir, they're official. I didn't make them up.

ANDREI. Oh, where is it now, where's my past gone, eh? When I was young, and full of life, what's become of all those dreams and clever ideas, when my present and future were bright with hope? Why is it we become so dull, grey and uninteresting, when we've barely started to live? Why do we become lazy and apathetic, useless wretches . . . ? This town's been in existence now for two hundred years, with a hundred thousand inhabitants, and there isn't one of them any different from the rest, not a single great man, alive or dead. Not one scientist or artist, or anyone of the least significance, that might arouse envy, or a passionate desire to emulate him . . . All they do is eat, drink, sleep, and eventually die . . . Others are born, and they too eat, drink, sleep, and so as not to die of boredom, bring some variety into their lives with vicious backbiting, vodka, gambling, and lawsuits. Wives betray their husbands, and the husbands lie, and pretend they see nothing, hear nothing, while their vulgarity irresistibly influences the children, crushes the life out of them, extinguishes the divine spark, till they become just as pathetic, just as corpse-like, as their mothers and fathers . . . (*To* FERAPONT, *crossly.*) What is it you want?

FERAPONT. What? These papers have to be signed.

ANDREI. You're getting on my nerves.

FERAPONT (*hands over the papers*). The porter at the finance office was telling me just now . . . he says, last winter in St. Petersburg they had two hundred degrees of frost.

ANDREI. I detest the life I lead now, but when I think about the future, well, that's something else! Everything seems so airy and bright, I can see a glimmer of light in the distance, I can see freedom, I can see myself and my children free, too – free from idleness, from perpetual stale beer, and goose and cabbage, from after-dinner naps, from all this vulgar dependency . . .

FERAPONT. Yes, they say two thousand people froze to death. Folks were scared stiff, they say. Either Petersburg or Moscow, I can't remember.

ANDREI (*overwhelmed with tenderness*). Oh, my dear sisters, my darling sisters! (*tearfully.*) Dearest Masha . . .

NATASHA (*at the window*). Who's making all that noise out here? Is it you, Andrei? You'll waken Sophie. *Il ne faut pas faire du bruit, la Sophie est dormée déjà. Vous êtes un ours.* (*Getting annoyed.*) If you want to talk, give the pram to someone else. Ferapont, take the pram from the master!

FERAPONT. Yes, ma'am. (*Takes the pram.*)

ANDREI (*embarrassed*). I was talking quietly.

NATASHA (*cuddling her little boy at the window.*) Bobik! Naughty Bobik! Who's a little rascal?

ANDREI (*looking over the papers*). All right, I'll look through these and sign what's necessary, then you can take them back to the council. (*Goes into the house, reading the papers.* FERAPONT *wheels the pram upstage.*)

NATASHA (*at the window*). What's Mummy's name, Bobik? Who's Mummy's clever boy! And who's that? That's Auntie Olya, say 'Hello, Auntie Olya!'

Some wandering musicians, a man and a girl, enter playing a violin and a harp. VERSHININ, OLGA *and* ANFISA *emerge from the house and listen a moment in silence.* IRINA *goes up to them.*

OLGA. Our garden's like a public thoroughfare, everybody uses it. Nanny, give these musicians something.

ANFISA (*gives the musicians some money*). God bless you, my dears.

The musicians bow and leave.

Poor things. You don't have to play round the streets if you're well fed. (*To* IRINA.) Irina, love! (*Embraces her.*) Oh, my darling girl, if you could see me now! What a life I have! I'm living in a school flat now with my lovely Olya – that's what the good Lord's granted me in my old age. I've never been so well off, old sinner that I am . . It's a big flat, there's no rent to pay – it's school property, you see – and I've got my own little room and bed. I wake up at night sometimes, and I think, oh, Holy Mother of God, I must be the happiest person in the world!

VERSHININ (*glancing at his watch*). We'll be leaving soon, Olga. It's time I was going.

A pause.

I wish you all the very best . . . Where's Masha?

IRINA. She's in the garden somewhere|. . . I'll go and find her.

VERSHININ. If you would, please. I'm in a hurry.

ANFISA. I'll look for her too. (*Shouts.*) Masha! Masha, dear! Coo-eee! (*Exits with* IRINA *to the far end of the garden.*) Coo-eee! Coo-eee!

VERSHININ. Well, all good things come to an end. And here we are, saying goodbye. (*Looks at his watch.*) The town threw a sort of official lunch for us. We had champagne, and the Mayor made a speech. I ate and listened, but my mind was elsewhere – here, with all of you. (*Looks round the garden.*) Yes, I've got so used to you.

OLGA. D'you think we'll see each other again?

VERSHININ. Probably not.

A pause.

My wife and my two little girls'll be staying on here for another month or two. Please, if anything should happen, or if they need . . .

OLGA. Yes, yes, of course. Don't worry.

A pause.

By tomorrow, there won't be a single officer left in the town – only memories. And we'll be starting a new life, of course.

A pause.

Nothing ever turns out the way we'd like. I didn't want to be a headmistress, but that's what I've become. That means I won't be going to Moscow.

VERSHININ. Anyway . . . Thank you for everything . . . I'm
   sorry if there's anything I've done . . . I've talked a lot,
   I know – far too much. Forgive me for that, and don't
   think ill of me . . .

OLGA (*wiping her eyes*). What on earth's keeping Masha?

VERSHININ. What else can I say to you before I go? What
   can I philosophise about? . . . (*Laughs.*) Yes, it's a hard life.
   To many of us it seems hopelessly dreary, but you must
   admit it's gradually getting easier, and clearer, and the
   time isn't far off when it'll shine out like a beacon. (*Looks at
   his watch.*) I really ought to be going. Yes, in the old days,
   mankind was obsessed with war, our entire existence was
   taken up with campaigns, invasions, victories – now that's
   all old hat, but it's left behind a great void, clamouring to
   be filled. Mankind is passionately searching for something,
   though, and we shall find it. But it can't come too soon, for
   me. (*Pause.*) If we could only find a means of injecting
   some culture into work, and some hard work into culture!
   (*Looks at his watch.*) I really must go . . .

OLGA. Here she comes now.

   MASHA *enters.*

VERSHININ. I've come to say goodbye.

   OLGA *walks a little way apart, so as not to inhibit their
   leavetaking.*

MASHA (*gazing into his eyes*). Goodbye. (*A prolonged embrace.*)

OLGA. Stop it, stop . . .

   MASHA *sobs bitterly.*

VERSHININ. Write to me . . . Don't forget! Please, let me go, it's time . . . Olga, take her, please, I have to go . . . I'm late . . .

Deeply moved, he kisses OLGA's *hand, then embraces* MASHA *once again and hurriedly exits.*

OLGA. Masha, that's enough. Please don't, darling . . .

KULYGIN *enters.*

KULYGIN (*embarrassed*). Never mind, let her cry . . . Oh, my dearest Masha, my dear, good Masha . . . You're my wife, and I'm happy, no matter what . . . I'm not complaining, I wouldn't dream of reproaching you. Olga here is my witness . . . We'll go on living the way we used to, and I won't say a word, not a hint of blame . . .

MASHA (*restraining her sobs*). 'By a curving shore stands a green oak tree, bound with a golden chain . . . Bound with a golden chain . . . ' I'm going mad . . . 'By a curving shore . . . A green oak tree . . . '

OLGA. Masha, calm down . . . Please . . . Give her some water.

MASHA. No, I've stopped crying . . .

KULYGIN. She's stopped crying . . . She's a good woman . .
.

In the distance, the muffled sound of a shot.

MASHA. 'By a curving shore stands a green oak tree, bound with a golden chain . . . A green cat . . . A green oak . . . I'm getting all mixed up . . . (*Drinks some water.*) My life's ruined . . . I don't want anything . . . I'll be all right in a minute . . . It doesn't matter . . . What does that mean, a curving shore? Why do those words keep going through my mind? My thoughts are all mixed up.

IRINA *enters.*

OLGA. Masha, calm down, please. That's better, there's a good girl . . . Let's go inside.

MASHA (*angrily*). I'm not going in there. (*Begins sobbing, but stops almost immediately.*) I don't go in there any more, I'm never going back into that house . . .

IRINA. Let's just sit out here together, without speaking. You know I'm leaving tomorrow . . .

KULYGIN (*after a pause*). Look, I confiscated these whiskers from a lad in the Third Form yesterday. (*Dons a false beard and moustache.*) I look like our German teacher, don't you think? (*Laughs.*) They're so funny, those boys.

MASHA. Actually, you do look like the German teacher.

OLGA (*laughs.*) Yes, you do.

MASHA *starts crying.*

IRINA. Masha, don't . . .

KULYGIN. Just like him.

NATASHA *enters.*

NATASHA (*to the* MAID). What? Oh yes, Mr Protopopov'll look after little Sophie, and the master can take Bobik out in the pram. Really, children are so much bother . . . (*To* IRINA.) Irina, you're leaving tomorrow – what a shame. Why don't you stay a few more days? (*Catching sight of* KULYGIN, *she lets out a shriek.* KULYGIN *laughs and takes off the false beard and moustache.*) Oh you – you gave me such a fright! (*To* IRINA.) You know, I've got so used to you, it's not going to be easy saying goodbye to you, believe me. I'll have them move Andrei into your room, along with his fiddle – he can saw away in there! – and I'll put little Sophie into his room. She's such a delightful child, an absolute angel. You know, she looked up at me today with her darling little eyes, and said 'Mama!'

KULYGIN. She's a beautiful child, that's true.

NATASHA. So, tomorrow I'll be on my own. (*Sighs.*) The first thing I'll do is cut down that avenue of fir-trees, then the maple . . . it looks so ugly at nights . . . (*To* IRINA.) Really, my dear, that sash doesn't suit you at all . . . It looks awful, you need something a bit brighter. And I'll have flowers planted everywhere, lots of them, for the perfume . . . (*Sternly.*) What's this fork doing on the bench? (*Walks up to the house, shouting to the* MAID.) I want to know – what's this fork doing on the bench! (*Shrieks.*) Shut up!

KULYGIN. She's off again.

In the distance, a military band is playing a march. Everyone listens.

OLGA. They're leaving.

CHEBUTYKIN *enters.*

MASHA. Our men are leaving. Well . . . *Bon voyage* to them! (*To* KULYGIN.) We'd better go home . . . Where's my hat and cape?

KULYGIN. I took them inside . . . I'll go and fetch them. (*Goes into the house.*)

OLGA. Yes, we can all go home now. It's about time.

CHEBUTYKIN. Olga Sergeyevna . . .

OLGA. What is it? (*Pause.*) What's the matter?

CHEBUTYKIN. Nothing . . . I don't know how to tell
you . . . (*Whispers in her ear.*)

OLGA (*horrified.*) No, it's not possible!

CHEBUTYKIN. I'm afraid so . . . A nasty business . . .
I've had enough, I'm sick of it all . . . I don't want to talk
about it . . . (*Testily.*) Anyway, what does it matter?

MASHA. What's happened?

OLGA (*puts her arms round* IRINA). This is a dreadful day . . .
Oh, my dear, I don't know how to tell you . . .

IRINA. Tell me what? What's happened? What is it? For the
love of God, tell me! (*Starts crying.*)

CHEBUTYKIN. The Baron's been killed in a duel . . .

IRINA (*quietly weeping.*) Oh, I knew it, I knew it . . .

CHEBUTYKIN (*sits down on a bench upstage*). I'm worn out . . .
(*Takes a newspaper out of his pocket.*) Well, let them cry for a
bit . . . (*Sings softly.*) 'Ta-ra-ra boom-dee-ay, ta-ra-ra boom-
dee-ay . . . ' Does it really matter?

The three sisters are standing with their arms around each other.

MASHA. Just listen to the band playing. They're leaving us,
one of them's already gone, gone forever, and we're left
alone, to begin life over again. We must live . . . we must . . .

IRINA (*lays her head on* OLGA'*s bosom*). One day . . . one day
people will know what all this was for, all this suffering,
there'll be no more mysteries, but until then we have to

carry on living . . . we must work, that's all we can do. I'm leaving by myself tomorrow, I'll teach in a school, and devote my whole life to people who need it. It's autumn now, it'll soon be winter, and there'll be snow everywhere, but I'll be working . . . yes, working.

OLGA (*embraces both her sisters*). The band's playing so cheerfully, and I want to live so much! Oh, dear Heaven . . . Time will pass, and we'll be gone forever, we'll be forgotten, they'll forget our faces, our voices, even how many of us there were. But our sufferings will turn into joy for those who come after us, peace and happiness will reign on earth, and we who live now will be remembered with a kind word, and a blessing. No, my dear sisters, our lives aren't over yet. We must live! The band plays on so cheerfully, so joyously – it's as if any minute now we'll discover why we live, and why we suffer . . . Oh, if only we knew! If only we knew!

The music fades gradually into the distance. KULYGIN *enters in high spirits, smiling, carrying* MASHA*'s hat and cape.* ANDREI *wheels Bobik past in the pram.*

CHEBUTYKIN (*sings quietly*). 'Ta-ra-ra boom-dee-ay, ta-ra-ra boom-dee-ay . . . ' (*Reads his newspaper.*) What does it matter? What does anything matter?

OLGA. Oh, if only we knew! If only we knew!

Curtain.